Jo KEARNEY

How to Get the Job
You Want
in Hawaii

by
Rich Budnick

How to get the job you want in Hawaii

Published by

Aloha Press
Box 4183
Honolulu, HI 96812

Library of Congress Catalog Card Number 98-93432
    Budnick, Rich
    ISBN NO. 0-944081-03-7

Book cover design by Debra Castro, INform Graphic Design, Inc.
illustrations from Nova Development Corporation

Acknowledgments

Many people in many professions offered their wisdom, insight, and experience to this book.

The author wants to acknowledge the contributions of:

Lynn Miller, Karin Ireland, Ken Roberts, Lianne K. Maeda, Nadine Stollenmaier, Dave Saurer, Stacy Hasegawa, Cherlyn Logan, Debra Castro, Wilfredo Tungol, Kristine Bucar, Naomi Harada, Beverly Marica, Chuck Braden, Bob Sigall, Lynn Nakagawa, Cathy Heflin, Jeannie Thompson, Pamela Gottlieb, Jim Dote, Sybil Kyi, Bob Watada, Alvin Tanaka, Norma MacDonald, Blayne Hanagami, Blas Silva, Carol Pregill, Tim Lyons, Dick Botti, Hyan Pae, and Jackie Pang.

A special thanks also to my wife, Min-Tzu Hsiao Budnick.

Table of Contents

Introduction

Mark-up this book as you read it!

Go ahead, use your pen, pencil and highlighter. Make notes and highlight the dozens of tips and lessons that will help you get the job you want, faster than you ever thought possible.

This book takes the guess work out of job hunting by showing you how to plan your way to success. Job hunting is a skill you can learn, not a matter of luck.

During my work with the State Labor Department, I had the opportunity to meet many public and private sector job placement specialists, career planners, and personnel professionals. They offered many ideas about how to get a job in the real world.

This book is the result of attending job search seminars and conferences, interviewing personnel experts as well as job seekers, and engaging in personal research to verify what was learned.

Now it's your turn. There's practical information here that you can use immediately.

Especially helpful is the 74-page list of Hawaii's 1,600 top companies that employ nearly two-thirds of all workers in dozens of industries.

How to Get the Job You Want in Hawaii will help you get the job you want, at the company where you want to work.

Planning your career

Your first job

Are you looking for your first job? If so, you are probably a student, a recent graduate or a homemaker entering the workforce after many years of caring for a family.

Or perhaps you've worked for the same company for many years, and now you're looking for a new job.

As a new job seeker, you're probably nervous because you lack experience in job hunting: calling and meeting employers, writing a resume, and answering tough job interview questions.

This book will give you the confidence you need, and teach you the skills to get you the job you want.

What every job seeker should know

Everyone who applies for a job should be concerned with:

▶ Your appearance and hygiene
▶ Your attitude
▶ The information you submit in a cover letter, resume, and job application
▶ The job interview: what you say and how you say it
▶ The people you offer as your personal references

What kind of career do you want?

Think about your strengths, abilities and interests, what you like and dislike. It's never too late to make a career decision. A career counselor can guide you toward a career or occupation that you will enjoy.

 You can identify the career or job you want by taking classes or attending seminars to learn a new skill. Doing volunteer work for a non-profit agency will give you experience in the occupation that interests you.

What kind of job do you want?

The public library has many books about jobs, occupations and careers, including:

▶ CAREER KOKUA OCCUPATION BOOKS 1 AND 2, published by the State Labor Department. Provides detailed information about more than 300 Hawaii occupations representing 90% of the jobs in Hawaii. Learn about job descriptions, qualifications, salary, employment outlook, etc.

▶ DICTIONARY OF OCCUPATIONAL TITLES, published by the U.S. Department of Labor. Two volumes, with 1,400 pages, describe more than 12,000 occupations nationwide.

▶ OCCUPATIONAL OUTLOOK HANDBOOK, published by the U.S. Department of Labor. Describes 250 major jobs representing about 85% of the national workforce. Learn about job outlook, salaries, skill requirements, education and training, and more.

Job training programs

The Yellow Pages of the phone book list many business and trade schools offering specialized skill training and education in dozens of professions.

For information about government-funded job training and apprenticeship programs in Hawaii, contact:

Employment Training Center
University of Hawaii
33 S. King St.
Honolulu, HI 96813
phone 832-3700

Oahu
Work Hawaii
715 S. King St. #500
Honolulu, HI 96813
phone 523-4102

Kauai
Kauai Community College
30-1901 Kaumualii Hwy.
Lihue, HI 96766
phone 245-3210

Maui
Hawaii State Labor Department
Workforce Development Division
2064 Wells St. #108
Wailuku, HI 96793
phone 984-2091

Hilo
Hawaii State Labor Department
Workforce Development Division
180 Kinoole St.
Hilo, HI 96720
phone 961-7481

Kona
Hawaii State Labor Department
Workforce Development Division
74-5565 Luhia
Kailua-Kona, HI 96740
phone 326-2855

How to prepare for a job layoff

Today, few people spend their entire working life at the same company. Most people change jobs several times...and you may even change career fields once or twice.

Start planning your job search now if you:

► Expect to be laid off
► Get fired
► Dislike your current job
► Prefer another job that offers better pay, benefits, working conditions, advancement or location
► Want to pursue another career

What if you lose your job?

If you lose your job, a brief period of unemployment can be a good time to think about where you've been and where you're going. It's called "taking one step back in order to take two steps forward."

► Do you want to change careers?
► Do you want to learn new job skills?
► Do you want to attend a trade school or college for a certificate or degree?
► How long can you keep paying the bills before you must get a part-time or full-time job?

Should you quit before finding another job?

You may be fully justified in quitting your job. What if:

- ▶ You are mistreated on the job
- ▶ You are continually overworked
- ▶ You are underworked and bored
- ▶ No one listens to you or takes your advice
- ▶ You are reprimanded unnecessarily
- ▶ Your boss is an idiot or a monster to work for
- ▶ You know you could do better elsewhere

Are you desperate to quit your job today? If so, would you be better off unemployed? The grim reality is that you are usually better off looking for a new job while you stick it out at your current job.

 It's easier to get a new job while you have a job. Why? Employers would rather hire someone who's gainfully employed.

There's another good reason for hanging in there. If you quit, you'll be unemployed. Maybe you'd like a couple of weeks to rest. But what if the weeks drag into months? Now you'll take any job. You're desperate. Yipes! You need money to pay the bills, and your savings are running out. You might become so desperate you'll take your horrible, old job back.

Can you "grin and bear it" at the lousy job until you find another job? No matter how much you hate your current job, a period of long-term unemployment is likely to be more stressful than any amount of suffering you are now experiencing at a job you hate.

 If you are unemployed and earning income from a hobby or if you've established a small part-time business, you should tell potential new employers that you are self-employed.

If you're going to be fired or laid off

Sometimes you can see it coming. You've heard rumors, or you sense that something is wrong. If a lay-off is coming, try to find out in advance if you will be affected. Plan ahead to protect yourself and prepare for your future.

Losing your job is a traumatic experience – do what you can to minimize the suffering and help yourself get ahead.

Try these options:

▶ When you meet with your boss to discuss your firing or lay-off, act like a professional. This is no time to argue, cry, or beg for another chance. An emotional outburst won't help your case. Take good notes, even if it means asking your boss to repeat his statements so you can be accurate.

▶ If you can, negotiate for a better severance package than the company is offering. Try to get benefits such as: lump-sum pay; company paid health insurance; company-supported assistance to find a new job; financial assistance for job training, or education classes to gain new skills or improve your current skills.

▶ Before you sign a waiver of your rights to future actions against the company, make sure you receive a satisfactory severance settlement and reference letter in your hands.

▶ Talk to your supervisor about getting a friendly or supportive reference letter. If necessary, draft a letter for your supervisor to sign.

▶ If you are leaving on less than happy terms, get your boss to agree that the company will merely state your job title and dates of employment – and he won't say anything negative to a potential employer who calls for a reference. This is something you have little control over, but at least you can try.

► Look at your personnel file and copy anything that might benefit you.

► Check if you are protected by any state or federal civil rights laws. For instance, are most of the people at your company being laid off from a certain ethnic, age or gender group? What's the company history of layoffs? This may not help you keep your job, but it may help you negotiate a better severance package. If you think the company is discriminating, you may want to hire a labor attorney or file a complaint with a government agency.

► Apply for Unemployment Insurance as **soon** as you are out of work. Unemployment benefits begin during the second week after you file for unemployment. Then it takes another 3-4 weeks to receive your first unemployment check. Reminder: Workers don't pay to the Unemployment Insurance fund, employers do!

► Discuss your situation with your family, and begin looking for a job immediately!

► Plan your personal finances. Pay your bills, prepare a spending plan, delay making large purchases, and talk with your creditors. Surprisingly, many creditors will probably agree to rearrange your payment schedule for a while. You may need at least six months of savings in your bank account.

 **JOB TIP** Don't burn your bridges. Try to leave your job on happy, friendly terms. If you hate your boss, try not to show it.

Whether you decide to find another job or if you think are going to lose your job, you can prepare yourself by:

▶ Contacting people about a new job
▶ Taking classes or attending seminars to upgrade your skills or to learn new skills
▶ Attending workshops to learn about new career opportunities

Cheerful people get jobs faster

You're not the only one...
Unemployment can happen to anyone

This chapter is intended for people who are unemployed, and don't have the "luxury" of job hunting while they still have a job.

If you're out of work longer than you expected, you're probably thinking that you're the only person in the whole world who doesn't have a job. Be assured — you aren't alone. There are lots of people in the same predicament as you. Many of the world's most successful corporate executives are out of work right now, looking for jobs.

How to cope with the stress of unemployment
...and the stress of finding a job

People who are cheerful and upbeat tend to get hired sooner. If you think it's difficult to be constantly cheerful while you're unemployed, consider this: If you had to choose between two equally qualified candidates, would you hire a cheerful person or someone who complains about how hard it is to find a job?

When you're looking for a job, you've got to believe in yourself, and have confidence in your abilities. Your immediate goal is to get a job.

You are responsible for your actions. If you don't have an active job search plan, if you don't knock on doors and make phone calls, no one's going to call you.

The more you push yourself to succeed, the faster you will.

Are you having difficulty adjusting to the emotional stress of unemployment? Are you sitting at home all day, worrying about not earning money? Are you worried you won't get a job?

It doesn't take long for reality to set in. The longer you are unemployed, the more frustrated, angry and troubled you will feel.

However "low" you are feeling now, you will feel great when you finally get the job you want. In fact, some people look back on their unemployment and admit it was a blessing in disguise because it opened the door to a new career, or a better job with better pay.

Long term unemployment is stressful. It affects your health, and how you get along with people...including potential employers. Worrying starts in your head and moves to your stomach. You feel it in your pocketbook too. Your unemployment check offers temporary income, but it won't pay all the bills.

You can overcome unemployment stress by keeping busy looking for a job and staying optimistic. Treat your job hunting activity as if it were a job. Make it a full-time activity.

How can you be optimistic if you're feeling lousy about being out of work? Believe in yourself, that's how. There's a brighter day ahead. If these words sound hollow, look at the facts. You will get a good job eventually, won't you? Of course you will.

Every failure brings you a step closer to success

While trying to make the first electric light bulb, America's great inventor Thomas Edison said he wasn't discouraged that he had failed with 1,000 different filaments. Heck, no. He said he was

1,000 filaments closer to success because he knew which ones didn't work.

During your job search, you will experience many disappointments before you succeed. The good news is: the more "no's" you get, the closer you are to "yes."

If you're lucky, your job search may look like this:

no no no no yes

However, don't be surprised if your job search looks like this:

no no no no no no no no no no no no no no no
no no no no no no no no no no no no no no no
no no no no no no no no no no no no no no no yes

The more times people say "no," the closer you are to "yes."

The more contacts you make, the faster you will get the job you want. If you fear losing confidence by getting so many rejections, try to think like a salesperson. A salesperson doesn't sell at every attempt, especially in the beginning. It takes time to learn the territory, the product, the message, and the skills of selling.

Salespeople often suffer countless rejections for every sale they make. They overcome rejections all day, every day. Likewise, you will probably experience many rejections before you get the job you want.

Be like Edison...or be like a salesperson. Keep a positive attitude and hang in there, despite the obstacles and disappointments.

 JOB TIP

You must persevere without fear of failure. Remember, failure is a pit stop on the road to success.

How to handle disappointment

After suffering a string of disappointments, many job seekers get stuck in paralysis — a common job hunting disease called "do nothing-itis." You sit at home and do nothing. You worry about past mistakes and failures. You replay in your mind what went wrong at your last job, and what you could have done to change things.

What's worse, you may feel like a loser because, without a job, you're now on the outside looking in. You know you have talent, but you are unrecognized, unrewarded and jobless.

Hey, wake up! Fight off "the blahs" and avoid "do nothing-itis." Don't fall into this rut — stick to your goals and focus on the future. Get off the couch. You've got work to do. Start making phone calls. Start typing, printing and mailing letters. You'll achieve success tomorrow from what you accomplish today.

Remember, a lot of employers are going to say "no" before you hear that magic word, "yes." Keep your ego focused on that one "yes" you're waiting for.

You have two hurdles to overcome:

▶ Handling disappointment
▶ Making a list of employers to contact, and doing it

A tale of two job seekers: Joe Lee and

Are you like Joe Lee?
If so, be aware of your emotions

Joe Lee was a happy-go-lucky guy until he struggled through a full year of unemployment. The first few weeks were productive and restful. He made lists of people he knew, and told them he was looking for a job. He read the newspaper ads, applied for numerous jobs, and had a few good interviews. Suddenly, time ran out. Joe's vacation pay and unemployment insurance came and went.

"Is my career over? Do I have a future?" Joe asked himself.

After reading the want ads in the morning, he'd turn on the TV to cheer himself up. He'd cruise the channels. "Nothing's on," he'd say, and shut the TV.

He ate junk food even though he wasn't hungry, and gained unwanted weight, which he thought about every time he opened the refrigerator.

Restless, sure, yet he rarely found time to exercise. He was too depressed to try to motivate himself to feel good. To relax, he'd lie down on the couch and take a brief nap.

Joe suffered through the roller coaster of emotions. Sometimes a rejection letter in the mail would set off angry outbursts, but it didn't make him feel any better.

Joe used to enjoy the time he spent at home on weekends, holidays and vacations. Now, he never felt more alone than the time he wasted away at home, in his "prison," unemployed. He couldn't stand being alone with his negative thoughts.

Joe thought he'd tried everything to get a job, but so far, nothing has worked. He's not a quitter, so he still replies to newspaper ads and asks his friends if they've heard about any job openings.

"Oh well," he sighed, "There are good days and bad days." When the bad days come, Joe felt helpless, hopeless, and useless.

Denise Albano...   How do you compare?

Are you like Denise Albano?
She succeeded with patience and persistence

Denise lost her job when her company was acquired by a larger company.

"Oh, oh," Denise thought "what will I do?" She took a few days to settle herself down, then dug in for a fight. She threw herself head first into a battle to find a good job. "This is war," and I have to win!" she told herself over and over.

Job hunting as war? Few wars are won in a single battle. Most take time to win.

After a couple of months, Denise began feeling discouraged. How long will it take? She'd had a few job interviews from the newspaper ads, but no luck there.

Denise told everyone she was looking for a job, and asked them to refer her name to anyone who might want to hire someone with her skills.

She called people she didn't know, and made appointments with business leaders in her field. To get her foot in the door, she inquired about general career opportunities, rather than a specific job. Denise maintained a very busy schedule of telephoning people. She tried to get at least one appointment a day.

Denise worked very, very hard. It was the hardest work she'd ever done, and it was emotionally draining, too. Some of the interviews were productive, while others led to dead ends.

"Whew," Denise confided in a friend, "it's hard to be upbeat all the time, but I am playing a 'role.' I've learned to project a happy personality during every interview."

By chance, someone knew someone who suggested Denise to the department manager of a mid-sized company for a soon-to-be vacant position. This was the opportunity Denise had been patiently yet persistently working toward. Bingo, Denise got the job she wanted!

"I deserve it," Denise told her friend. "I'm qualified, and I worked very hard to get it!"

Now ask yourself a single question:

► What can you do to motivate yourself **right now** to look for a job?

Don't let your emotions control your life

When you're unemployed, the feelings of anger, sadness, frustration and job envy may lead to occasional anger and depression. You will experience good days and bad days. Depression can be like quicksand. It's hard to get out of it once you fall into it.

**JOB TIP** It always helps if someone can cheer you up, encourage you to "put on a happy face," and push you when you need it. Your family and friends can help by offering encouragement, not criticism during your difficult times.

When you're unemployed, a busy job search effort is the remedy for idleness. Looking for work is a full-time job. The more time you spend looking for a job, the faster you'll get the job you want.

Take charge of your life by planning daily and weekly job hunting activities – and stick to your plan, no matter how long it takes. If you have a plan, you're more likely to stay on track, and avoid getting sidetracked when you feel discouraged.

Force yourself to write letters and make follow-up phone calls. When people say "no," don't take it personally, and don't be discouraged. It may take countless letters, phone calls, and job interviews before you get the job you want. The more rejections you get, the closer you are to success!

If you're feeling in a rut, and don't feel like making phone calls, you can avoid "do nothing-itis" by telling yourself that you'll make just one call. That's right, just one phone call. Once you've made the call it was easy, wasn't it? Now give yourself just 10 minutes for two more calls. Now you're in a groove, and you're motivated to continue making phone calls for an hour or so.

Make a daily list

Keep active. Stick to a schedule so you don't waste a lot of time. Make a list of things to do every day, and note what you've accomplished.

To prepare for the new day, think of what you need to do before you get out of bed in the morning. Stay in bed until you get one or two ideas. Now get up and write them down. Next, check the day's list of things to do.

By continually making a list of things to do, you're motivating yourself to follow through.

A daily schedule gives you a sense of purpose and direction. It reminds you of what you must do. Planning ahead gives you something to look forward to. It keeps you optimistic, enthusiastic and productive. As they say in the business world, "if you fail to plan, you're planning to fail."

Reach out and renew acquaintances

Don't be embarrassed about being jobless, and don't avoid people. By reaching out to people, you will find new job leads. Make a list of friends, former co-workers, and acquaintances you've recently met. Start calling them. Ask them to tell you about job opportunities they hear about. If you don't ask, you won't get job referrals. Through networking, you will get the job you want.

People are more likely to help you if you show them a positive and cheerful attitude.

Where to meet people

Meet people at civic clubs, sports activities, religious groups, community organizations, or through professional or union associations.

Be a volunteer

A good way to help yourself is to help others. Volunteer for a charity, a non-profit group, a business or professional organization. As a volunteer, you will keep your skills sharp, learn new skills, and expand your opportunities to get a job through the people you meet.

Budgeting: Involve your family in your plans

Talk with your family about how everyone can spend less money. Tell them there is less money coming home, so they must pinch their spending habits until you get another job. Set up a 3-6 month budget based on your reduced income, and discuss how everyone can set priorities on what they spend. Do you have any other financial resources you can tap, such as relatives or a profitable hobby?

If necessary, notify your creditors. If you fail to notify them, and you stop making payments, you may face their wrath. They might take you to court, sue you, or hit you with very high interest charges. On the other hand, creditors can be lenient and understanding if you notify them in advance. Ask for a new, partial payment schedule that allows you to pay less than your regular payments. You will be surprised at how cooperative creditors can be.

 If you've recently lost your job, apply for Unemployment Insurance with the State Labor Department. You may also qualify for medical coverage with the State Health Department, or food stamps and other services with the State Department of Human Services.

Hobbies and recreation

Don't sit around and mope. Find time for hobbies and get regular physical exercise to help you relax, clear your head, and do what you enjoy doing. Take a daily walk, go fishing, make crafts, or learn a new skill, etc.

Typical barriers to employment

Let's be realistic. When you look for another job, you may face obstacles, such as:

- ► I'm too young...they're hiring people with more experience
- ► I'm too old...they're hiring younger, entry level people
- ► I'm overqualified...they're hiring entry level people
- ► I lack specialized skills and experience
- ► There aren't any jobs available in my field
- ► There are too many workers in my occupation
- ► I don't know what kind of a job I want
- ► I've had too many jobs...employers are afraid that I will leave for another company
- ► They're not hiring people of my (race, ethnicity, gender)
- ► I am unable to speak or write English well
- ► I lack reliable transportation
- ► I lack reliable child care
- ► Former employers may give me a poor recommendation
- ► I will have to explain health problems

Monthly budget
while you're looking for a job

Income

Unemployment income
Spouse's income
Severance and Vacation Pay
Interest/Dividends
Stocks
Other income
    Hobbies
    Business
Savings Accounts
Insurance Cash Value

Total Income

Expenses	Typical	Reduce to	Comments
Mortgage/Rent			
Maintenance/Repairs			
Property taxes			
Property insurance			
Services (yard maintenance, etc.)			
Utilities			
Phone			
Electric/Gas			
Water			
Sewer			
Cable TV			
Food			
Restaurants			
Groceries			
Miscellaneous			
Transportation			
Car Payment			
Car Insurance			
Gas			

Expenses	Typical	Reduce to	Comments
Taxi			
Bus			
Other Loan Payments			
_____			
_____			
_____			
Health Care			
Medical Insurance			
Dental Insurance			
_____			
_____			
Drugs			
Other Expenses			
School			
Tuition			
Child Care			
Clothes			
Entertainment			
Recreation			
Newspapers/Magazines/Books			
Income Taxes			
Life Insurance			
Investments			
IRA			
Charities			
Credit Card Payments			
Other Payments			

Total Expenses

Total Income
Less Total Expenses

Balance

How do you cope with, and overcome these barriers? Emphasize your strengths, and be prepared with a good explanation for any potential barriers. For instance:

- ✓ ▶ If you are over age 40, emphasize your experience, maturity and stability
- ▶ If you are just out of school, say that you are a fast learner and enthusiastic
- ✓ ▶ If you are lacking certain skills, explain that you are willing to attend classes or seminars to gain those skills
- ✓ ▶ If you lack exactly the experience the employer wants, explain how your volunteer work relates to this job. Always be positive and cheerful. Employers like that.

Some final tips about being unemployed

JOB TIP

Every resume you mail, every phone call you make, and every person you meet will contribute to your ultimate success. One success leads to another. With hard work, you make your own luck

---

To get a job, it will take:

- ▶ Time
- ▶ Patience
- ▶ Persistence
- ▶ A plan that you stick to
- ▶ Resourcefulness
- ▶ Networking
- ▶ Self-confidence
- ▶ Learning job search skills

The 15 most common ways to get a job

Why people get hired

There are many reasons why one person is hired over another:

▶ You have priority job rights at the company where you work
▶ The hiring manager knows you
▶ The hiring manager likes your personality
▶ The hiring manager has a positive "gut feeling" that you'll do a good job or you'll "fit in"
▶ You were referred by the right person
▶ You have the right skills and experience
▶ You have excellent recommendations
▶ You are seeking the salary the company is willing to pay
▶ You are enthusiastic and cheerful

Employers hire people for many reasons, including "gut feeling" and "feel good" instincts. When dozens of qualified people apply for the same job, it can be difficult to determine who is the best qualified. If you can demonstrate that you are the best candidate, you'll get hired.

 **JOB TIP**
Consider doing something that will catch the hiring manager's attention.

Here's an example of what a less-qualified applicant did to get a job against hundreds of more qualified applicants. He needed a "hook to set himself apart," so he wrote his own letter of recommendation. He explains his method:

> "I responded to an ad in the newspaper. There was a big response, 700 resumes for a single job in sales — many from people who had better qualifications than me. So I wrote a glowing recommendation letter, and in the last paragraph, I admitted that the person writing the recommendation was me. The letter made me stand out, got me in the door, and helped me get the job."

Recommendation letters make a good impression

Get a recommendation letter from every boss you've ever had. The letter should state your job title, dates of employment, your job description, and your strong points. If you don't have such a letter, call your former bosses and ask for one. If any former boss says he's busy, offer to draft a letter — he can always edit it and sign it. If you've had a boss that you didn't get along with, find something that you can agree on, and limit the letter to that.

If you're being fired or if you're quitting your present job on difficult terms, try to negotiate a recommendation letter. Get a promise that if a potential employer calls, your supervisor will only confirm the dates you worked, your job title, and your job duties. You can't expect an unhappy supervisor to mention your strong points, can you?

Many employers check references, so try to minimize any potential problems that a reference check may reveal.

The 15 most commonly used job search strategies

Tell people you are looking

Do you know: **half** of all jobs are found through word of mouth? People often get hired because someone knows you from somewhere. It could be a professional, social, sports, religious or ethnic connection, or simply because you are someone's neighbor, relative, or former school classmate. Or maybe you sat next to someone on the bus...or an airplane flight.

 **JOB TIP**
Tell everyone you can think of that you are looking for a new job. Ask people if they know any company with a job opening. Personal referrals and word of mouth are the fastest ways to get the job you want.

Read the newspaper ads

The good news is: newspaper ads list hundreds of job openings. You should respond to these ads immediately. However, the bad news is: newspaper ads represent only 20% of the actual job openings. Be aware that you are competing with dozens or hundreds of people who are reading the same newspaper ads.

Professional organizations or labor unions

Look in the Yellow Pages of the phone book for business and trade organizations, associations, and labor unions.

Join a professional organization and attend meetings. You will meet people and learn about job openings in your profession. Networking helps! Plus, some professional organizations send resumes of job seekers to large companies.

If you are a union member, ask that your name be placed on a union job list so you will be notified about job openings.

At professional association meetings, people have been known to stand up and announce: "I am looking for a job." You might get a job referral...or an interview!

When you attend professional association meetings, make an active effort to meet as many people as you can. Collect their business cards. Follow up with a phone call reminder of your recent meeting.

Private employment agencies

Private employment agencies help hundreds of people find jobs in Hawaii each year. In most cases, the employer pays for this service, not the job seeker.

Private employment agencies receive scores of job listings that employers don't want to place in the newspaper – especially for jobs in administrative, clerical, financial, technical and scientific occupations.

Don't send your resume to every employment agency in town. Call first, and ask if they receive many job orders in your profession.

Executive search firms

Executive search firms, also known as "headhunters," specialize in professional jobs, usually high-paying executive positions. Employers pay "headhunters" to find candidates to fill very specific jobs.

Temporary help agencies

Temporary agencies "rent" workers on a short-term basis to employers. Such jobs can last from one day to several months. Temporary jobs can lead to permanent employment. Most temporary agencies fill office-related and health care jobs.

Companies

Most people send mass letters to the company president or personnel office, hoping for a job. This is a waste of time, energy and postage stamps. Call, write or make an appointment with the person who actually does the hiring for your position.

Contact the department or hiring manager, not the personnel office. The personnel office rarely does the hiring, and usually "cleans out" its files every few months. Don't expect the personnel office to call you when there's a job vacancy.

Yellow Pages of the phone book

The Yellow Pages list thousands of companies, in hundreds of categories. Identify the companies you'd like to work for, and contact the hiring manager of each company.

The media:
newspaper stories, business and professional magazines

Be alert for stories about new companies, business expansions, and new hiring. There might be a job vacancy when an employee was promoted, or when someone left a company for another. Business newspapers, trade and professional magazines and newsletters may list job openings or feature a special column about people who have been recently hired or promoted.

College placement offices

Each year, college job placement offices help students and alumni find jobs.

Professional resume writers

Professional resume writers can help you present or "sell" yourself on paper, so you will make a good impression with employers. A professionally-written resume will clarify what you do – your skills, experience, accomplishments, etc. Check the Yellow Pages under "Resume Services."

Career counselors

Private career counselors provide testing or counseling services that will help you identify your skills and interests. They may create a personal job search plan for you to follow.

Volunteer

Many people find the job they want after volunteering with non-profit organizations, social service agencies, political causes, charities, etc.

Volunteering is a great way to meet people, work at something you enjoy doing, gain work experience, learn a new skill, and build a network of contacts that can lead to job referrals.

 **JOB TIP** People of all ages volunteer as a way of deciding what kind of career they're interested in. Think of volunteering as if you were "scouting" for a job. Many people who are unemployed make time to volunteer as a way of networking for job referrals.

If you already have a full-time job, you can volunteer on weekends or evenings.

Many students work at public or private sector jobs through "Internship" programs. As compensation for their labor, interns receive either a small wage or class credit. Internship programs provide an invaluable learning experience.

It is not uncommon for a large agency or company to hire past interns for permanent jobs. If you're a student, and you want to "get your foot in the door," consider interning for a company or nonprofit agency. As an intern, you gain "insider" status when an entry-level job becomes available. Since the hiring manager knows you, the job may be yours for the asking!

Job Searching via the Internet

The Internet is growing in popularity, and becoming increasingly useful in helping you get the job you want.

You'll find thousands of Web sites offering helpful career resources, job vacancies, and information about employers. You can even post your resume on the Web, but be careful how much personal information you reveal!

Check out "Hawaii Careers" – a free, online Web site Internet resource for job seekers and employers.

Hawaii Careers is divided into several sections that include "hyperlinks" to other World Wide Web sites related to employment in Hawaii.

One section provides "links" to hundreds of job opportunities through the Web employment pages of Hawaii employers. Other sections include links to Hawaii employment agencies that have Web sites. Links are also provided to Web sites of local recruiters, placement agencies, and some local online classified sections.

Plus you'll find information about labor laws and programs from the State Labor Department, and several business organizations.

Since the goal of Hawaii Careers is to help people find jobs, there are pointers to other like-minded Web sites such as "Hawaii Jobs" and "Pacific Information Exchange's Pointers to Employment."

It's free: government agencies

Federal, state and local government personnel offices list job opportunities. Call or visit their personnel offices.

For a list of government employment offices, see the list of Hawaii's 1,600 top employers.

Visit the State Labor Department

The State Labor Department helps thousands of people find private sector jobs each year through the Workforce Development offices. You can obtain free job referral and job placement services, and information about government funded job training programs.

Honolulu
830 Punchbowl #112
Honolulu 96813
586-8700

Waipahu
West Waipahu Center
94-275 Mokuola Street #300
Waipahu 96797
675-0010

Kaneohe
45-1141 Kamehameha Hwy
Kaneohe 96744
233-3700

Maui
2064 Wells Street #108
Wailuku 96793
984-2091

Molokai
75 Ala Malama St
Kaunakakai 96748
553-3281

Kailua-Kona
Kaiwi Square
74-5565 Luhia St, Bldg C, Bay 4
Kailua-Kona 96740
326-2855

Hilo
Kaiko'o Mall #121
777 Kilauea Ave
Hilo 96720
974-4136

Kauai
3100 Kuhio Hwy #C-10
Lihue 96766
274-3056

A faster, better way to get a job

Finding the "hidden jobs"

Job searching is a **skill** that you can master.

Whenever possible, you should bypass the company personnel office and go directly to the department or hiring manager – that's the key to getting the job you want – by finding the "hidden jobs" through the people who make the hiring decisions.

What's a hidden job? A hidden job is any vacancy that's not advertised in the newspaper. Think of it as an "insider" job that you can apply for before anyone else does. That's where you'll find the most job opportunities.

Think of someone you know who keeps advancing up the career ladder because he knows a lot of people. Whether you call it the hidden job market, networking, or guerrilla job hunting – it's very effective in landing jobs at a faster rate than relying on newspaper ads.

If luck is being in the right place at the right time, then you've got to meet as many people as you can. You create your own luck by tapping into the hidden job market, and getting referrals to job openings.

Treat everyone you meet as a potential contact for your job hunting efforts. People will tell you about job openings only if they know you're looking for a job.

Wake up job hunter! It's a myth to believe that all or most jobs are advertised in the newspaper. Reading the newspaper ads is the slowest and laziest way to look for a job. Newspaper ads reveal just the tip of the iceberg.

 Newspaper ads are often the last step an employer takes to fill a job. It may surprise you, but as many as 75% of all job openings are filled **without** being advertised in the newspaper.

Most people make the mistake of spending **all** of their energy:

► Reading and responding to the newspaper classified ads
► Contacting company personnel offices
► Contacting employment agencies and executive recruiters
► Mailing mass resumes to employers

In theory, the more resumes you mail, the more responses you will receive, and the better your chances to get a job. Baloney!!! Few companies will respond to your mass mailing. If anything, you'll get a "Dear John" form letter from a handful of personnel offices, with a polite message: "We have no job openings now, and we'll keep your resume on file...."

Don't hold your breath waiting for a phone call. You've just wasted a lot of time, energy, and money on postage and printing.

 Avoid mass mailings! Avoid the personnel office — they may have good intentions, but they don't make the final hiring decisions. If you're waiting for the newspaper ads, you're putting all your eggs in one basket.

To succeed, you've got to develop your own leads. The opportunities are out there...and you've got to create them.

Your goal is...

▶ To find employers before they advertise the job
▶ To interview for jobs before a vacancy exists

A job interview is a face-to-face meeting with an employer, even if there is no job vacancy.

The hidden jobs are everywhere

About two-thirds to three-fourths of all jobs are "invisible" – that is, they aren't advertised in newspapers or listed with employment agencies.
Here's what happens:

1. Most employers first look to promote someone from within the company.

2. If no one in the company is qualified...or interested...many employers ask their friends, professional associates, and co-workers for names of qualified people to interview for a vacant job. A handful of people may be referred.

3. Then, if no one is hired from the hidden job market, the employer will buy an ad in the newspaper, resulting in dozens or hundreds of job applications.

An employer who buys a newspaper ad has to answer the phone calls, open the extra mail, read a huge pile of resumes and carefully select a handful of job applicants to call for an interview. Then he's got to set aside his regular work for 1-3 days to interview these people. Finally, someone's got to type and mail dozens of "regret" letters.
If you were the hiring manager, you'd be overwhelmed, wouldn't you?

Hey, wake up job seeker! The hidden job market is faster and more effective. It's better to be among the few than to be buried somewhere in the pack.

Whenever possible, most employers prefer to select from a few qualified, pre-screened applicants referred by colleagues through the hidden job market.

That makes sense, doesn't it?

You're seeking career advice, not a job

How many times have you called someone and asked for a job — only to be told the company has no job. The conversation ends quickly, doesn't it? You ask for a job and they start thinking, "I don't have any job openings and I'm too busy to waste time with someone I don't know."

Once you tell employers that you're seeking career advice, not a job, they will relax, and many will find time for you — especially if someone they know has referred you to them.

You're not asking for a job because you know they probably don't have one. The advantage of tapping into the hidden job market is that you are establishing a personal network of referrals through "information interviews." You are meeting and gaining the confidence of hiring managers, and getting interviews without asking for a job.

 **JOB TIP** An information interview is where you ask for information and advice about a profession or industry, or how a manager became successful. You'll meet people who make the hiring decisions, and that's the way to get the job you want.

You're getting your foot in the door, and who knows, sometime soon they might have a job opening — or they'll know someone who does, and ask for a referral. Guess who they're likely to call? Someone they know: You.

Finding a job through the hidden job market will get you more interviews, and it's a lot faster than relying solely on newspaper ads that everyone reads.

During your search for hidden jobs, you will gain many inside tips and practical advice. You'll find potential employers, uncover opportunities, and lay the foundation for getting the job you want.

Getting interviews is what job hunting is all about.

Obtaining information interviews requires time and effort to: send individual letters, make phone calls, and meet numerous people.

 **JOB TIP** To get the job you want, you're not taking the haphazard, mass mailing "shotgun approach," you're aiming carefully at a very specific target, one employer at a time.

The advantages of having a plan

Begin your quest with a plan, and stick to it. People who have a plan are less likely to get sidetracked by temporary disappointment. Have the patience and persistence of the salesman and the scientist.

 **JOB TIP** Having a plan makes you better organized, better prepared...and puts you in a position to win. With every rejection, you are one interview closer to getting the job you want.

From now on, when you contact hiring managers, you'll be asking them for career information and advice, not a job. Remember, if you ask for a job, they probably don't have a job vacancy, and they'll be too busy to talk to you.

By asking for information and advice, you are appealing to the hiring manager's ego to share his wisdom, experience, and path to success. He may feel like a mentor by telling you about his work.

Advantages of using the hidden job market to obtain information interviews

▶ You will get job interviews, job leads, and job offers faster
▶ You will receive honest advice and job leads from successful people
▶ You aren't competing against anyone – and you're improving the odds in your favor
▶ You are interviewing for a job long before it is available or advertised
▶ Your information interview may actually be a preliminary job interview
▶ You are meeting people who make the hiring decisions
▶ You are interviewing with many companies in a relatively short period of time
▶ You are networking: meeting employers, getting referrals and interviews via referrals
▶ You are improving your resume by getting advice from the managers who hire people in your field

---

How do I get started?

You should begin by contacting:

▶ People you know: professional peers, friends, relatives, neighbors, etc.
▶ People who may refer you to other people. Referrals make it easier to get appointments.
▶ People you meet.
▶ People you read about: Check the newspaper columns about newly-hired people. Call or write them and say you read about their recent appointment, and you'd like to know how they became successful.
▶ People from a list of companies that hire people with your skills. Call hiring managers you don't know, and ask them how they became successful.

A job is just a phone call away

When you look for a hidden job, you're just a phone call away from getting the job you want!

Are you afraid of making phone calls for fear of rejection? The worst that can happen is that your phone call will take less than a minute and an employer will say "no."

Can you make 10 phone calls in an hour? If so, you can probably get an information interview. Try to get 1-2 interviews a day — that's 5-10 interviews a week or 30-60 a month. That's a much greater success rate than if you responded to newspaper ads.

How to gain courage to make phone calls

You may feel comfortable calling friends or relatives, but now you've got to call strangers for job appointments and interviews, to get referrals and job leads.

Some people have a difficult time calling strangers, but you can overcome this if you:

▶ Play the role of an actor
▶ Have a script to follow, and practice in advance
▶ Tell yourself you have to make the calls because you need a job to pay the bills

Here's what to say to the hiring manager

When you get the hiring manager on the phone, be brief. Say something like:

"Hello, I am _____. My friend Michelle Tavares of ____ Company suggested I call you. I'm not calling to ask for a job — but I am looking to make a career change. I'd like to ask you for some information and advice about the ___ profession/industry and how you became successful. I'd need only about 20 minutes of your time."

Hold your breath and wait for a response. If he says "yes" – set the date for a meeting. If he hesitates, remind him that you're not asking for a job. If he says "no" – ask if he can suggest someone who you could call to learn more about the ____ industry or profession.

Advice for sending information letters

If you prefer to send a letter to the hiring manager before calling:

▶ Write to a specific person
▶ Identify who referred you
▶ Emphasize that you are **not** asking for a job
▶ Identify your skills and why you are writing:
    ▶ You are considering new career opportunities
    ▶ You want to learn more about his industry or profession, or how he became successful
    ▶ You'd like about 20 minutes of his time to get some advice
▶ Close with a thank you, a promise to call, and when
▶ Personalize your letter so it doesn't read like a form letter
▶ Make no errors: proofread out loud
▶ Use 8 1/2" by 11" white or ivory paper with laser quality print; or a good typewriter ribbon

When you follow-up with your phone call, tell the secretary you are calling about "correspondence" you sent. The hiring manager may not remember your letter, so remind him that you had promised to call, which is what you are doing now.

When you get to your information interview

When you meet an employer for an information interview, remember: you're not going to ask for a job. You don't expect that he has one anyway! Be an actor. Know what questions to ask, and be truthful in your role. You are the interviewer, not the job seeker.

Learn as much as you can about the hiring manager, his com-

How to get past the secretary

Call and ask for the name and title of the person who's in charge of the _____ department (which employs people with your skills).

Many secretaries are protective of their bosses, so it's important to speak in a matter of fact tone of voice. Say:

▶ "I'm calling because _____ (a professional colleague the manager knows) advised me to call."
▶ "I'm updating my files...or sending correspondence." Ask how the boss' name is spelled. Then ask if he's the hiring manager. Don't say you're looking for a job.
▶ "I'm seeking information about ___ topic that relates to _____ (your profession)." That's another way of saying: "I'm seeking career information, not a job."

If the person you want to talk to is never in, try calling before 8 a.m. or after 5 p.m. Many hard-working bosses start early and work late. Some even work at their desk through lunch.

If you can't get past the secretary after a couple of calls, give your name and say: "It's about a previous phone call," which it is, since you called earlier.

Be polite, and confident. If you hit a stone wall, say "Thank you, I'll call back later." Call again in a few hours or the next day — when the secretary won't recognize your voice. If you still can't get through, then call the person who referred you, and ask that person to call for you. That's a real plus!

If you previously sent the hiring manager a letter, this is your follow-up phone call. Ask to speak with the department manager by name. If you are asked what the call is about, you can say: "I'm calling about correspondence," since you already sent a letter.

pany, his occupation, and his industry. It's okay if the interview takes a bit longer than the 20 minutes you asked for. However, be mindful of the time, and don't overstay your welcome.

Introduce yourself, identify who referred you, and state **clearly** that you are seeking career advice, **not** a job.

1. When you get to your information meeting, say: "Thank you for meeting me. Michelle Tavares said I should meet you because I am interested in exploring career alternatives in the _____ profession/industry..."

2. At the beginning of your meeting, give some personal information about yourself if you are asked — or save it for near the end. Don't spend more than a minute or two talking about yourself.

Questions to ask at your information interview

Open-ended questions give the employer an opportunity to elaborate. You don't have to ask all of the questions listed here, so be flexible. Be enthusiastic and show interest. It's important that you be a good listener, not a big talker. You want to make a favorable impression with the hiring manager!

- ► How did you get started?
- ► What do you like about your job and other jobs you've had in this profession?
- ► What specific jobs fall in this field?
- ► What are the job requirements: education, skills, and experience?
- ► What are the job-related responsibilities, problems and opportunities?

sample letter

Sam Chinn
P.O. Box 83
Honolulu, HI 96812
(808) 555-1111

date

Mr. Joe Hamada
Rainbow Hotel
88 Aa St.
Honolulu, HI 96813

Dear Mr. Hamada:

Michelle Tavares of Aloha Hotel suggested I contact you for career advice about the accounting profession and the hotel industry, and how you became successful. I am not asking you for a job, but I am looking to make a career change and I'd appreciate some wise counsel about career opportunities.

I'd like to know which of my restaurant bookkeeping skills are transferable to the hotel industry. My strengths are in accounts receivable and payable, payroll, tax reports, bank deposits and reconciliations, inventory reports, daily sales journals, financial statements and annual budgets.

– or if you're a recent graduate –

I have recently graduated from college with a degree in business, and I am researching career opportunities in several industries. I'm a fast learner, creative, and excellent with details.

I will call you on ___ to schedule a meeting at your convenience.

▶ What is the salary range?

▶ What are the duties of different jobs within the broad occupation?

▶ What are the career opportunities and job turnover?

▶ What is the potential of this company or unit, and industry?

Don't rush to talk about yourself, except in an introductory way. If the employer asks you to explain something about yourself, go ahead, but be brief. If you spend more than 1-2 minutes talking about yourself, the employer may think that you **will** ask for a job — and that defeats the purpose of your information interview.

After explaining a little about yourself, be sure to inform the employer that you are hard-working, honest and capable of doing the kind of job he's been talking about. Then ask these questions:

▶ Would I qualify for such a job?

▶ If I don't qualify, what am I lacking?

▶ What transferable skills do I have?

▶ How you can overcome any objections that potential employers may have?

The importance of getting names as the information interview ends

When you think your interview has about 5 minutes left, point out that you have learned a lot from the manager's advice, and ask for the names of other employers to contact — not for a job, but for an information interview.

This is the **#1 goal** of your interview. Why? Because you want to get the names of other people you can interview. You will call them and say, "so and so from such and such company suggested I call you..." Referrals make it much easier to get an interview.

Like the branches of a tree, one person suggests two or three people for you to call. Each of those two or three people may suggest two or three more people, and so on. Pretty soon, you're building a large and effective job search network. Someone is apt to refer you, or to call you about a job.

As you're ready to leave, casually give the employer a copy of your resume, and say, "Here's a copy of my resume, just for your reference."

Always ask for a business card of the person you've just interviewed.

That's it!

If you don't leave your resume...

Some professional career advisors discourage you from leaving your resume at the information interview. They feel it creates the impression that you sought the meeting to ask for a job. If you don't leave your resume, leave a business card. When you send a thank you letter, include your resume and ask the manager if he'd take a few minutes to look at it and make suggestions to help you.

After the information interview

▶ Send a "thank you" letter the same day or the next day. Look at the manager's business card for his correct name spelling and title. Your letter adds a touch of professionalism and leaves a positive impression with the manager you interviewed.

▶ Keep good records and files of your information interviews.

▶ Follow up and stay in touch — call him once in a while to ask for other names of people you can contact — or to share what you've learned in other information interviews.

What about blue collar and manual labor jobs?

Career counselors teach this technique with extraordinary results. It can work for you too.

For blue collar and manual labor jobs that don't require a formal resume − you should tell the hiring manager that you are looking for a job. You need not ask for career advice.

When you get the hiring manager on the phone, tell him what your skills are, and ask for a job. If he doesn't have any job openings, tell him that you'd like to discuss future opportunities. If you are asked to send a resume, do so **only** if there's a current job opening.

Don't call to say you heard about a job, and ask to come in right away for an interview. Always ask for the interview at the employer's convenience, not yours.

Who are you competing with? No one! The opportunity is yours. Hiring managers will admire your courage. Yes, it really works. You will have disappointments, but you'll find more success than you ever thought possible.

When you're making phone calls...

When you're busily making lots of phone calls, how can you expect people to return your call if they keep getting a busy signal?

If they don't know you, they will probably stop calling after the first try.

What can you do?

▶ You will need an inexpensive answering machine to record messages when you're out, or on the phone.

► You could get an extra phone line to make calls, but that is more costly. However, if you're looking for a good job, it may be worth the expense.

► Call the phone company and ask for advice. One option is a device that beeps when you get a call. Another records your messages when you're on the phone — so callers will never get a busy signal.

As technology improves, there will be other options to consider.

Sample thank you letter

Sam Chinn
P.O. Box 83
Honolulu, HI 96812
(808) 555-1111

date

Mr. Joe Hamada
Rainbow Hotel
88 Aa St.
Honolulu, HI 96813

Dear Mr. Hamada:

I enjoyed our meeting today, and appreciate your advice about the role of public relations in the insurance industry.

As I explained, I am seeking new career opportunities and searching for the right business or organization that can benefit from my skills, creativity and experience.

You may refer my name if you hear of any job opportunities where my public relations skills could benefit an employer.

I will stay in touch with you if I have any questions in my search for the "ideal" career. Thank you for offering to provide further advice from time to time.

Cordially,

Sam Chinn

How to write a resume and cover letter

When you apply for a job by submitting a resume and cover letter, you hope this happens:

1. You want the employer to read your cover letter and say: "This is a well-written letter. I'd like to read the resume."

2. You want the employer to read your resume and say: "This is an impressive resume. I want to interview this person."

 A well-written cover letter and resume will open the door to a job interview.

A resume lists your job qualifications, skills, experience, accomplishments, education and training – not necessarily in that order.

How to respond to a newspaper ad

► Your cover letter and resume should list the qualifications and experiences identified in the ad. It doesn't hurt to say you have all the skills the ad is seeking. Many personnel staff who receive and "screen" the resumes will check for every "key word" they list in the ad!

► Some ads ask for a "wish list" of qualifications and experiences that may be impossible to meet. You never know if they'll take someone less than perfect, so it's best to list whatever you've done that is relevant to the job you're seeking.

Cover letter

Always send your resume with a well-written cover letter. Your cover letter should be neat, identify what job you are applying for, and why you are qualified. Limit your cover letter to 2-4 paragraphs.

Modify your cover letter for each employer. An effective cover letter states how your skills, experience, education, and accomplishments will benefit the company.

A cover letter also highlights information that is not on your resume, or information that you want to emphasize.

Employers will read your cover letter first, and if they are interested, they will look at your resume. If you blow it with a sloppy cover letter – with a single typing or grammatical error – don't expect an employer to look at your resume!

Tips for cover letters:

- ▶ Use standard letter-size white or ivory bond paper
- ▶ Address each letter to a specific person
- ▶ Mention the name of the person who referred you
- ▶ Be brief
- ▶ Use short sentences and short paragraphs
- ▶ Be enthusiastic and positive
- ▶ Explain how your skills and experience match the employer's needs, and how you will benefit the company
- ▶ Urge the employer to act: ask for an interview
- ▶ Proofread the letter for spelling, grammar, and punctuation

Sample cover letter

Kenneth Perez
110 Mahalo St.
Honolulu, HI 96825
phone 222-3333

date

Dear ____:

I am applying for the Conference Coordinator position that you advertised. I enjoy working with people and planning special events.

Last year I organized four successful quarterly conferences for a bank, with more than 300 people participating in each one.

My responsibilities included directing all the planning and budgeting, inviting the guest speakers, managing the direct mail, gaining publicity, arranging for meals, etc. I coordinated and supervised the entire program, aided by a small staff.

I am proud to say that my assignments are completed on time, and within budget. I have a lot to offer in the way of enthusiasm, good ideas and ability.

I look forward to an interview at your convenience. Excellent references are available upon request.

Sincerely,

Kenneth Perez

How to write a good resume

Picture a stack of resumes piled high on a desk. Now picture someone reading the resumes. He's tired of looking at boring resumes, and probably regrets advertising to fill the vacant job. Your resume is probably buried somewhere in the middle.

On the average, each resume gets less than a minute to make a good impression. Most resumes look alike, and surprisingly, many applicants are unqualified for the job.

Fortunately, a few resumes stand out from the pack. When you're competing with dozens of job seekers, it's important to make your resume easy to read, clear, and to the point.

 A resume documents factual information. You could be fired if it is later discovered that you lied or misrepresented yourself. Be honest. You can clarify anything "sensitive" at your job interview...or when you are offered the job.

Resume Do's and Don'ts:

Few employers will "read" your entire resume. They will scan it quickly in a few seconds. If you want to look good to a potential employer, your resume must look good, too.

Do's:

▶ Make it easy to read
▶ Type or print your resume on letter size, 20 lb. white or ivory bond paper
▶ Make sure your resume is neat, clean, and attractive to look at
▶ Start your sentences with action verbs, not the word "I"

- ▶ Use short, simple sentences
- ▶ Impress the reader that you have the right experience, job skills and accomplishments, and that you are capable of accepting responsibilities
- ▶ If you lack experience, emphasize that you are a fast learner
- ▶ Modify your resume for each employer
- ▶ Limit your resume to 1-2 pages
- ▶ Proofread for spelling, punctuation and grammar
- ▶ Ask someone to proofread and review your resume

Don'ts:

- ▶ Don't say anything negative
- ▶ Don't misspell words
- ▶ Don't make any punctuation or grammatical errors
- ▶ Don't use technical jargon unless it will be understood by the employer
- ▶ Don't abbreviate words
- ▶ Don't provide excessive information about your skills and experience that is irrelevant to the job you are applying for
- ▶ Don't fail to account for time gaps between jobs
- ▶ Don't give false or misleading information
- ▶ Don't submit a resume that's too long or too short
- ▶ Don't submit a resume that's poorly typed or poorly photocopied
- ▶ Don't print your resume on fancy paper
- ▶ Don't give irrelevant personal information: height, weight, age, gender, race, hobbies, health, family background, religious affiliation, marital status, etc.
- ▶ Don't list your salary, your reasons for changing jobs, your supervisors' names and titles
- ▶ Don't list if you quit or were fired

 **JOB TIP**

If you are using a computer, don't use more than one typeface for your resume. If you want a few words of text to stand out, use bold, but don't overdo it. Use italic sparingly, if at all.

Oops!!!
Proofread your cover letter and resume

Mistakes happen, and that's too bad for you. You've missed your chance to get a job. Don't expect an employer to be sympathetic if there's a typing error or a computer error that you didn't catch.

Almost everyone uses computers with a "spell checker," so it seems ironic that misspelling and typing errors have increased. Why? People are over confident. You may be inserting an extra letter or word in the wrong place, or highlighting and eliminating the wrong part of the line. Oops, it takes just one simple keystroke to destroy your chances for a job.

Your spell checker won't distinguish the difference between correctly spelled words that are used incorrectly (e.g., than/then, affect/effect, to/too/two). Each of these words is spelled correctly, but only one is the correct word.

 It's faster to proofread your letter and resume directly on your computer screen, but you'll miss the errors unless you proof read the actual printed copy.

The actual resume

3 Resume formats

There are three basic resume formats:

- ▶ Chronological
- ▶ Skills – also called a Functional resume
- ▶ A combination of the two

Chronological resume

This is the most common resume and the easiest to write because it emphasizes your work experience. Personnel staff prefer it because it gives the basic chronological facts.

List your most recent job first, followed by all other jobs. You want to inform readers about what you've done, what companies you've worked for, the dates of your employment, and job duties.

Use a Chronological resume if:

► You are attending school or if you are a recent graduate
► You want to emphasize your work experience and job duties rather than your education, skills or accomplishments
► You are looking for career advancement, and you have been moving up the career ladder in your profession

Advantages:

► Easy to organize
► Shows your stable work experience in a way readers can follow
► Shows progress in your field

Disadvantages

► Employment gaps are easy to see
► There's little room to highlight your accomplishments or transferable skills
► It won't help if you want to change careers

Skills (Functional) resume

If you want to impress the hiring manager, a functional resume presents your skills and accomplishments first. It will take you longer to edit and rewrite, but it's worth the effort. Once you've completed a functional resume, you'll be impressed with your talents and achievements, and you'll know what skills are transferable to new careers.

Use a Skills (Functional) resume if:

▶ You want to emphasize your job skills and accomplishments rather than your work duties and places of employment
▶ You are changing careers
▶ You are experienced in your profession, a military veteran, an organization volunteer, or a homemaker with transferable skills
▶ You have gaps in your work experience
▶ You don't want to identify where you've worked

Advantages:

▶ Highlights your professional abilities, accomplishments and skills that the employer wants or needs
▶ Allows you to hide gaps in employment

Disadvantages

▶ Takes longer to organize and write well
▶ Places less emphasis on the names of companies where you've worked
▶ Needs to be customized for each employer

Combination resume

The combination resume looks like a functional resume, but it includes the basic information about your current and past jobs.

Use a Combination resume if:

► You want to highlight your skills and accomplishments, and also identify where you've worked.

Advantages:

► Information is more comprehensive
► May satisfy the needs of both personnel staff and hiring managers

Disadvantages:

► May be too lengthy
► Employment gaps stand out

Basic elements of a resume
(the order varies with a chronological, functional or combination resume)

► Basic personal information: your name, address and phone/fax
► Career or specific job objective (optional)
► Education:
   ► Formal degrees, certificates, licenses, etc.
   ► Workshops, seminars and conferences
► Work experience

- ▶ Skills and accomplishments
- ▶ Volunteer work experience
- ▶ Relevant professional, civic and charity experience
- ▶ Military experience
- ▶ Awards, recognition, and publications

 **JOB TIP** Always list the skills, accomplishments, experience and education relevant to the job you are applying for.

Personal information

- ▶ Your name
- ▶ Your address
- ▶ Your telephone/fax numbers: home and work, or where a message can be left

Occupation or career objective

The career experts are divided, so the choice is yours:

Many personnel staff who read your resume would like to see an occupation or career goal at the top of your resume: the job you are applying for or the ultimate career job you are seeking.

For example, if you are applying for a clerical job, you may want to say that you are pursuing a secretarial career that will eventually lead to a position as an administrative assistant or private secretary. If you are seeking a sales job, you may say that your career goal is to become a store manager.

On the other hand, many hiring managers don't care if you identify an occupation or career goal.

Education

If your work experience is limited, place your education near the top of the chronological resume. For a functional resume, list your education near the end because it is less important.

▶ Your last college attended, degrees received, major/minor subject specialization. If you didn't attend college, list your high school.
▶ If you are a recent graduate, list classes you took that are directly related to your employment objective
▶ Other education or training related to your occupational goals: conferences, seminars, workshops, correspondence courses, etc.
▶ Scholarships and honors you received
▶ Extracurricular activities (if relevant)
▶ Professional certificates or licenses

Work experience

List your **present or most recent job first, and work backward**. Provide:

▶ Dates of employment
▶ Employer's name and address, and type of business
▶ Your job title
▶ Describe your duties (emphasize the tasks which require the most skill, judgment, and responsibility). Include any specialization, special tools or equipment used, and special duties performed
▶ If you were a supervisor, the number of workers you supervised
▶ Briefly describe your accomplishments
▶ Your supervisor's name and title

Skills and accomplishments

You should emphasize not only what you've done, but how well you've done it. Identify your skills and accomplishments, and use action words to describe your experiences. Avoid using the word "I."

Highlight your accomplishments with dollar figures, percentages, or both. List any improvements you initiated or implemented, how much money you saved or produced, how you increased productivity, or any responsibilities you handled.

This may include:

▶ Statistical measures of performance or productivity – in percentages or dollars, such as:
  ▶ "Supervised the automation of the office filing system which yielded $2,000 in efficiency savings."
  ▶ "Improved the equipment maintenance program which reduced repair and replacement costs by 10 percent and saved $50,000 a year."

▶ Any recognition from management:
  ▶ "Received an employee of the month award."
  ▶ "Commended for coordinating the United Way charity campaign at the office."

▶ Problem solving activities:
  ▶ "Suggested solutions for faster processing of paperwork to improve customer service."

▶ Any other success stories:
  ▶ "Trained new staff."
  ▶ "Attained a perfect attendance record for three years without missing a day's work due to illness or injury."

 **JOB TIP** Entry level job applicants with little work experience should emphasize skills and accomplishments in school or with volunteer organizations. Add that you're always on time, work well with people, work without supervision, etc. Also mention any accomplishments, project teams you worked with, or leadership training you received.

Think of every job task as you highlight your skills and accomplishments in a functional resume. For instance, if you helped to organize a meeting, workshop or conference you may have been responsible for some of these job tasks:

▶ Budgeting all conference expenses and anticipated income
▶ Handling the money
▶ Planning the topics to be discussed and the speakers to be invited
▶ Inviting and scheduling all speakers
▶ Making arrangements for the room(s)
▶ Determining the food costs and coordinating meals with the hotel or caterer
▶ Identifying the amount of space necessary for the conference
▶ Writing, designing, laying out the promotional flyers
▶ Obtaining mailing lists for direct mail promotion
▶ Typing and organizing mailing lists
▶ Planning and overseeing the activities of volunteers who folded, stuffed and mailed flyers, and staffed the conference
▶ Writing press releases and public service announcements
▶ Gaining publicity by arranging for media interviews with prominent conference speakers, or giving the interviews yourself for newspaper, radio and TV coverage
▶ Coordinating the printing of the flyers and conference booklets by obtaining quotes from various printers
▶ Preparing the workshop booklet
▶ Staffing the registration table, preparing name tags for all speakers, participants and volunteers

These tasks may have required you to possess or use skills such as:

▶ Budgeting, accounting, bookkeeping, and handling financial transactions
▶ Communicating with business leaders and professionals
▶ Scheduling events and meeting timetables
▶ Establishing effective working relationships with people
▶ Writing, desktop publishing and graphic arts skills
▶ Motivating people
▶ Supervising people
▶ Delegating tasks to volunteers
▶ Developing ideas for a project and implementing them
▶ Exercising public relations, advertising and media skills

Now that you've read these lengthy lists, you've gained a new perspective of how to communicate your skills and accomplishments. From now on, when you are asked what you do at work, you won't say, "not much."

Volunteer work

As a volunteer, many of your volunteer experiences and skills relate to the corporate world. Review the above section on skills and accomplishments for ideas on how to communicate what you know, and what you've done.

If you lack formal job experience, include relevant volunteer work and highlight your transferable job skills. If you have no experience as a volunteer, get some! List your job title and describe what you did on the job, such as:

▶ Specific job duties
▶ Equipment used
▶ Skills learned
▶ Goods and services you produced
▶ Goals met

- ▶ Number of people you supervised
- ▶ Improvements you initiated or implemented
- ▶ How much money you saved or produced
- ▶ How you increased productivity

Relevant professional, civic and charity experience

List organizations that you belong to, and your specific accomplishments.

Military experience

Explain your skills in a way that a hiring manager can understand.

- ▶ Give military branch and length of service
- ▶ List your major duties, detailing those tasks related to the job you are seeking. Keep it simple and short.

Example:

| Military | U.S. Air Force, dates (month and year) |
| Service | aircraft mechanic |

Enlisted in the Air Force after high school graduation. Worked as a mechanic, specializing in engine repair and maintenance of various aircraft.

Awards and recognition

List any professional, civic or charity awards or recognition you have received.

References

List three references with names, addresses and phone numbers — or say that references will be provided upon request.

Ask people for permission to use them as a reference, and "if not, please tell me now." If they hesitate, don't use them. You don't want your reference to speak unfavorably of you. This embarrassing problem is more common than people realize.

Before you leave your job, negotiate with your employer for a reference letter or ask someone other than your boss. If you didn't get along with your boss, find something that you did well that he can mention in a letter. If necessary, draft a letter for your boss to sign.

Reason for leaving

Don't mention it on your resume.

175 Action verbs

How to describe your accomplishments, skills and experience in your cover letter and resume, and at your job interview

achieve	communicate	dispense	gather
address	compare	display	generate
administer	compile	distribute	govern
analyze	compose	draft	group
answer	conceive	draw	guide
apply	conceptualize		
appraise	conduct	earn	handle
approve	construct	edit	
arrange	contract	encourage	identify
assemble	control	enforce	illustrate
assess	convince	enlarge	implement
attain	coordinate	entertain	improve
author	correlate	equip	increase
award	correspond	establish	influence
	create	estimate	inform
balance	cut	evaluate	initiate
budget		examine	innovate
build	decide	execute	inspect
buy	define	expand	inspire
	delegate	experiment	install
calculate	demonstrate		institute
catalogue	design	fashion	integrate
clarify	detail	fix	interview
classify	develop	forecast	introduce
coach	devise	form	invent
collect	direct	formulate	investigate
		found	

judge	perceive	remodel	supervise
	perform	repair	support
lay out	persuade	research	synthesize
launch	pioneer	review	systematize
lead	plan	revise	
listen	prepare		tailor
	present	save	teach
maintain	prevent	schedule	train
manage	process	search	transform
market	produce	secure	translate
mediate	program	select	
meet	project	serve	unify
monitor	promote	simplify	unite
motivate	propose	sketch	use
	protect	sell	
negotiate	prove	solve	validate
	provide	sort	
observe	purchase	speak	verify
obtain		stimulate	write
operate	recommend	strengthen	
organize	record	structure	
originate	recruit	succeed	
overhaul	reduce	summarize	

Chronological Resume - Administrative Assistant

Jane Adachi
19 Aloha St.
Honolulu, HI 96822
(808) 555-1111

WORK EXPERIENCE

year-Current   Personal Secretary, HMG Direct, Honolulu, HI.
Secretary to the Marketing Director. Duties
include: Supervising a clerical staff of four;
word processing; developing a new filing
system; scheduling meetings; keeping a
calendar of promotional activities; making
purchases; making sure all deadlines are met for
submitting advertising to media representatives.

year   Secretary, ZYZ Stores, Honolulu, HI.
Secretary to Assistant the Personnel Director.
Duties included: Typing correspondence and
forms; proof reading legal documents; processing the mail; maintaining a filing system.

year   Clerk-Typist, MYM, Inc., Honolulu, HI
Duties included: Typing correspondence;
processing invoices and mail; establishing and
maintaining a filing system; answering the
telephone.

SKILLS   Word processing: Microsoft Word and Excel.
Typing 60 wpm.
Excellent organizational skills.

AFFILIATION   American Secretarial Association.

EDUCATION   A.A., Secretarial Science
Kapiolani Community College.

REFERENCES   Available upon request.

Skills Resume - Administrative Assistant

Jane Adachi
19 Aloha St.
Honolulu, HI 96822
(808) 555-1111

SKILLS and ACCOMPLISHMENTS

Supervisory: Supervised a clerical staff of four.

Organization: Developed a new filing system that increased efficiency and reduced time to find documents.

Purchasing: Saved $15,000 in annual interest costs by paying bills on time; familiar with procurement procedures.

Computer: Microsoft Word and Excel.

EXPERIENCE

year-Current   Personal Secretary, HMG Company, Honolulu, HI.
Secretary to the Marketing Director.

year   Secretary, ZYZ Stores, Honolulu, HI.
Secretary to the Assistant Personnel Director.

year   Clerk-Typist, MYM, Inc., Honolulu, HI.

TRAINING   Customer Service workshop.
Telephone Courtesy workshop.

AFFILIATION   American Secretarial Association.

EDUCATION   A.A., Secretarial Science
Kapiolani Community College.

REFERENCES   Available upon request.

Combination Chronological/Skills Resume
Administrative Assistant

Jane Adachi
19 Aloha St.
Honolulu, HI 96822
(808) 555-1111

WORK EXPERIENCE

year-Current	Personal Secretary, HMG Direct, Honolulu, HI. Secretary to the Marketing Director. Duties include: supervising a clerical staff of four; typing correspondence; ensuring all deadlines are met for submitting advertising to media representatives; scheduling meetings; keeping a calendar of promotional activities; and purchasing.
Achievements:	• Developed a new filing system. • Never missed a deadline for submitting advertising to media representatives.
year(s)	Secretary, ZYZ Stores, Honolulu, HI. Secretary to the Assistant Personnel Director. Duties included: Typing correspondence and forms; proofreading legal documents; processing the mail; maintaining a filing system.
Achievements:	Coordinated a skills training program through community colleges and vocational trainers, enabling 30 employees to upgrade their skills.
year(s)	Clerk-Typist, MYM, Inc., Honolulu, HI. Duties included: Typing correspondence; processing invoices and purchase orders; establishing and maintaining a filing system; answering the telephone.

Achievements: • Developed a new filing system that increased
                   office efficiency and reduced time to find
                   documents.
                 • Reviewed bill paying costs and created a more
                   efficient system which saved $15,000 annually.

year(s)   Receptionist, Aloha Wear Co., Honolulu, HI.
                 Duties included: greeting clients, answering
                 the telephone.

Achievements: Created a system for identifying types of incom-
                 ing phone calls, by using friendlier phone
                 message recordings which met the information
                 and referral needs of callers.

SKILLS   Microsoft Word and Excel.
                 Typing 60 wpm.
                 Excellent organizational skills.

AFFILIATION American Secretarial Association.

EDUCATION   A.A., Secretarial Science
                 Kapiolani Community College.

REFERENCES   Available upon request.

Chronological Resume - Entry level sales

Cynthia Kumu
877 Mahalo Way
Honolulu, HI 96826
(808) 333-6666

OBJECTIVE   Entry level, full-time sales position.

EDUCATION   Mahalo High School, Honolulu, HI.

WORK EXPERIENCE

year-Current   Part-Time Cashier/Sales Assistant, Jo's Department Store, Honolulu, HI.
Duties include: Handling cash and credit cards; assisting customers with product questions and purchasing; balancing register sales; preparing daily sales summary; and stocking shelves.

SKILLS   • Trained in using the cash register.
• Good speaking, reading and writing abilities.
• Get along well with co-workers.
• Handled up to 300 customer contacts a day in a busy retail department store.
• Processed as much as $30,000 in purchases daily.
• Handled cash, credit card and check sales transactions.

REFERENCES   Available upon request.

Combination Chronological/Skills Resume
Entry level sales

Cynthia Kumu
877 Mahalo Way
Honolulu, HI 96826
(808) 333-6666

OBJECTIVE   Entry level sales position.

EDUCATION   Mahalo High School, Honolulu, HI.
Completed Business Education courses.

WORK EXPERIENCE

year-Current   Part-Time Cashier/Sales Assistant, Jo's Department Store, Honolulu, HI.
Duties include: Handling cash and credit cards;
assisting customers with product questions and
purchasing; balancing register sales; preparing
daily sales summary; and stocking shelves.

**SKILLS and
ABILITIES**

COMMUNICATION Excellent speaking, reading and writing abilities.
Get along well with co-workers.
Received excellent evaluations from supervisors.

**CUSTOMER
CONTACTS**   Have had up to 300 customer contacts a day in a
busy retail department store.

HANDLE SALES   Processed up to $30,000 in purchases daily.
Handled cash, credit card and check sales.

HARD WORKING   Worked part-time during school and full-time
during summers and long holiday vacations.

REFERENCES   Available upon request.

Chronological Resume - Marketing Director

Kenneth Perez
110 Mahalo St.
Honolulu, HI 96825
(808) 222-3333

WORK EXPERIENCE

year-Current	Self-employed: Marketing and sales consultant. Research and write comprehensive marketing plans to increase client business, and improve customer satisfaction; write, edit and lay out brochures, newsletters, annual reports, and ads; write magazine articles; organized three conferences which attracted 100-150 people.
year(s)	Marketing Director, ZYZ Stores. Responsible for researching, writing and implementing comprehensive marketing plans to increase business, and improve customer satisfaction at five retail stores. Increased sales by 6%, profits by 10%; and reduced customer returns by 8%. Implemented a direct mail program which identified and targeted key markets and produced $200,000 in new business.
year(s)	Marketing Specialist, MYM, Inc. Wrote and laid out brochures, newsletters, flyers, and ads.
COMPUTER	Microsoft Word and Excel, PageMaker, Quicken.
EDUCATION	B.A., History, University of Hawaii.
REFERENCES	Available upon request.

Skills Resume - Marketing Director

Kenneth Perez
110 Mahalo St.
Honolulu, HI 96825
(808) 222-3333

SKILLS and ACCOMPLISHMENTS

Marketing	Research and write marketing plans to identify and target key markets, increase business, and improve customer service; obtain reliable mailing lists to match prospects and products; establish a direct mail program that produced $200,000 in new business.
Sales	Received three "Salesperson of the Year" awards.
Advertising	Write, edit and lay out brochures, newsletters, flyers, annual reports, and ads which help clients increase business and improve their image.
Special Events	Organize conferences which attracted 100-150 people and earned 150% profits; responsible for hiring speakers; writing and mailing flyers; obtaining mailing lists; getting publicity.

EMPLOYMENT HISTORY

year-Current	Self-employed: marketing and sales consultant.
year(s)	Marketing Director, ZYZ Stores.
year(s)	Marketing Specialist, MYM, Inc.
year(s)	Salesperson, Aloha Wear Co.
COMPUTER	Microsoft Word and Excel, PageMaker, Quicken.
EDUCATION	B.A., History, University of Hawaii.
REFERENCES	Available upon request.

Combination Chronological/Functional Resume
Marketing Director

Kenneth Perez
110 Mahalo St.
Honolulu, HI 96825
(808) 222-3333

WORK EXPERIENCE

year-Current	Self-employed: Marketing and sales consultant. Research and write comprehensive marketing plans to increase client business, and improve customer satisfaction; write, edit and lay out brochures, newsletters, annual reports, and ads; write magazine articles.
Achievements:	• Organized three customer service conferences which attracted 100-150 people each. • Teach college non-credit workshops on business marketing and customer service for business organizations and colleges.
year(s)	Marketing Director, ZYZ Stores. Responsible for researching, writing and implementing a comprehensive marketing plan to increase business, and improve customer satisfaction for five retail stores.
Achievements:	• Increased sales by 6%, profits by 10%, and reduced customer returns by 8%. • Implemented a direct mail program which identified and targeted key markets, and produced $200,000 in new business.
year(s)	Marketing Specialist, MYM, Inc. Wrote, edited and laid out brochures, newsletters, flyers, and ads.

Achievements:	• Prepared a series of brochures which enabled MYM, Inc. to enter new markets with its products.
	• Prepared newsletters which resulted in creating and maintaining a database of repeat customers.
year(s)	Salesperson, Aloha Wear Co. Sold clothing to customers.
Achievements:	• Received "Salesperson of the Year" award three times.
COMPUTER	Microsoft Word and Excel, PageMaker, Quicken.
EDUCATION	B.A., History, University of Hawaii.
REFERENCES	Available upon request.

How to fill-out a job application

Many employers use a standard job application to determine if you qualify for a job. This gives employers a first impression about you – before they meet you.

Your job application should be neat, complete and accurate. If it is sloppy, incomplete or false, it makes a poor impression and you are not likely to be hired. False information may result in your immediate termination at any time.

If the application form doesn't allow enough space, ask the personnel manager where you can add more information.

Always take an extra resume with you. It's easy to copy the information from your resume to the job application. Give your resume to the employer.

Whenever you go to an employer's office to fill out a job application, bring a list of your previous employers, including:

- ▶ Company name
- ▶ Company address
- ▶ Company phone
- ▶ Name of your supervisor
- ▶ Employment dates (month and year)
- ▶ Job title
- ▶ Job description
- ▶ Beginning and ending salary

Here's how to make a good impression on your job application:

- ▶ Be brief and emphasize that you can do the work
- ▶ If you don't understand something: ask
- ▶ Check your application carefully for errors in spelling, punctuation and grammar

▶ Provide a telephone number for your home, work, and where a message can be left
▶ Don't say "see the attached resume"
▶ Fill out everything you are supposed to: don't leave any spaces blank. If necessary, you may write "Not Applicable" in the blank spaces.

Avoid the pitfalls of a job application

Job applications have two basic purposes:

▶ To screen people out
   – and –
▶ To find the best candidate

Don't put anything negative on your application. For example, don't say you were fired or were asked to resign from any job. If you mention it, you aren't likely to get interviewed. On the job application, it's better to say you left to take a job that:

▶ Pays more money
▶ Provides a better career opportunity
▶ Is a shorter commute from home to work
▶ Gives you more responsibility and more challenges
▶ Allows you a flexible schedule for child care or to attend school

A job application is a document of factual information. You could be fired if the employer discovers that you lied or misrepresented yourself. You can clarify anything "sensitive" at your job interview...or when you are offered a job.

How to prepare for the job interview

You have been invited to the job interview because you have the technical skills and other qualifications essential to the job. The job interview is the "persuasion stage," and you want to gain the "winning edge."

The interview has two purposes

As a nervous job seeker, you're probably sweating out the interview, unaware that it's a tough chore for the interviewer, too.

The hiring manager may be just as nervous as you! He may have just spent hundreds of dollars buying newspaper ads, and now he's worried that he might not select a good employee and he'll have to repeat the time consuming hiring process all over again.

Plus...the hiring manager is likely to be working late to finish his regular duties, because he's stuck giving job interviews. The hiring process drains an employer's time, money, and energy.

The employer may be interviewing 5-10 people who are equally talented, on paper, so he wants to pick the best job applicant. Sometimes the best person shines in the interview, and it's easy to make a selection. Other times, it's easier to dismiss all but one or two people through a process of elimination.

For the employer, the job interview has two purposes:

▶ To select the best person who "shines" in the interview
– and –
▶ To "weed out" who not to hire

As the job seeker, you may want to clarify anything "sensitive" that you did not explain fully in your resume or job application...or you can wait until you receive a job offer.

Why Hire Me?

The job interview is the most important part of getting a job. A good resume may help you "get your foot in the door," but the interview gets you the job.

You're competing with several people having comparable skills and experience, so here's your chance to prove yourself. You've got to convince an employer that you're the right person for the job, and you'll be good for the company.

 **JOB TIP** When you speak, give the employer a reason to hire you. The employer will judge your attitude, speaking ability, enthusiasm, and even though he won't admit it, he will judge your personality too.

An employer wants to know: why should he hire **you** instead of someone else?

► Are you as good as your resume implies?
► Are you competent?
► Will you create any problems?
► Will you be a "good fit" for the company?
► Will you "jump ship" and start looking for another job right away?

Research the company before the job interview

Most people who interview for jobs know very little about the company. You'll be ahead of everyone else if you spend some time researching the company before your job interview. Learn as much as you can about the company history, products and services, image, reputation, and accomplishments. This knowledge will help you relate your skills to the needs of the company, and the employer will be impressed with how much you know.

There are many ways to research a company:

- ▶ Go to the library and look for the company's annual report
- ▶ Call the company and ask their public relations office for an annual report or recent newsletters
- ▶ Search the Internet
- ▶ Call people who belong to a professional association
- ▶ Call the company and ask its employees why they like working there
- ▶ Call people who work for a competitor

Practice like an actor

Be careful what you say in the job interview, and how you say it.

The best way to prepare for a job interview is to be like an actor preparing for a performance: practice, practice, practice.

Find a friend to ask you typical interview questions, and critique your answers. Do it again and again until you **feel** comfortable, relaxed and confident. You want to **appear** smooth, enthusiastic, thoughtful and smart, but not rehearsed. You want to give the best possible answers in the best possible way.

Practicing prepares you:

- ▶ To handle any difficult or embarrassing questions without being defensive or negative
- ▶ It boosts your confidence
- ▶ It reduces the chance that you'll be caught off-guard
- ▶ It prepares you to do your best

Common problems that people experience while being interviewed for a job include:

▶ Sounding defensive, as if you are hiding something
▶ Being too wordy
▶ Speaking bitterly about your past employer
▶ Lacking enthusiasm

When you interview for a new job, you must leave behind any anger about your last job. Let your enthusiasm burst out. That's why practice interviewing is essential.

Hey, everyone gets fired. It doesn't mean you did a lousy job. Oftentimes the company has to cut somewhere, or you get caught in internal politics where you have no control.

You may be uncomfortable explaining what happened, so practice your answer so you don't sound defensive during a job interview.

Avoid saying:

▶ "Aaaaaaah"
▶ "And aah"
▶ "Well, aah"
▶ "Um"
▶ "And um"
▶ "It's like"
▶ "You know"
▶ "You know what I mean"
▶ "You know, da kine"

It's easy to be enthusiastic and full of hope during your first few job interviews. But the longer you're unemployed, the harder it is to be cheerful. You must continue to play the actor's role — even if you've experienced many rejections. Show a smiling "interview face," not a "worried face."

How to articulate your skills and accomplishments

As you prepare for your job interview, you should emphasize what you've done, and how well you've done it. Use action words to describe your experiences, skills and accomplishments.

Be prepared for untrained interviewers and illegal questions

Most employers have little or no training in how to ask questions, so they may not realize they are asking illegal questions. Federal and state laws prohibit employers from asking certain questions, especially about matters such as race, national origin, ancestry, religion, health, marital status, age, etc.

For instance, employers might ask an applicant about "receiving Workers' Compensation," "having children," or being "too young" or "overqualified" (i.e., having too much "experience" is another way of saying you are too old).

If that happens – don't jump up and shout, "It's illegal to ask that question!" Instead, you should:

▶ Ask how the question relates to your performing the job
    – or say –
▶ "I don't know that it's relevant to my job performance, but I can tell you..." Answer the question so it pertains to your ability to do the job. Then add how you have the skills to do what this job requires.
▶ If you think the question is illegal, just say the circumstance doesn't pose a problem, and you can do the job.

Some illegal questions may make you mad, but hold your temper or you won't be hired. Either the employer is being nasty, or he doesn't know he's asking an illegal question.

Questions can be carefully phrased to obtain the desired information legally. For instance, you can't be asked if you've received Workers' Compensation, but you can be asked if you've ever been hurt on the job.

When you get home, you can call the federal or state civil rights commissions.

Irrelevant questions

Interviewers from the personnel office often ask irrelevant questions, such as:

▶ What are your weaknesses?
▶ What did you like least about your last job?
▶ Where do you expect to be in five years?

The purpose of asking irrelevant questions is to see how well you answer them. This often creates a problem for people with little recent interviewing experience: first-time job seekers and people who've worked many years at the same company. If you take such questions literally and give literally honest answers, you probably won't get the job.

Always answer irrelevant questions in a roundabout way so you emphasize something positive, and make your weak points sound good.

 **JOB TIP** Never reveal any weakness or least-liked work activities. Never admit that you may continue looking for a better-paying job after you are hired for this job.

If an interviewer asks you something that you've listed clear as day in your resume, don't announce, "It's on my resume." An interviewer won't stop to look it up. Either the interviewer didn't do his homework and read your resume carefully — or he just wants to hear you answer the question.

You must give the personnel staff good answers or you won't advance to the job interview with the hiring manager.

Another problem with personnel is that they know little or nothing about the skills necessary to do many jobs, so they try to weed out people by asking questions that have no relationship to your ability.

More than a few department managers try to overcome this problem by asking the personnel office for a list of those applicants that personnel staff rejected, as well as the names of those who passed personnel's review. It's not uncommon for an applicant from the personnel office's rejected list to be hired.

Before the interview

▶ Allow enough time to get to the interview 10 minutes early. Allow for traffic problems, getting lost, finding parking, etc. If you arrive too early, take a walk. Many interviewers feel pressured and uncomfortable if you arrive more than 10 minutes early. If possible, drive by the company the day before, so you'll know exactly where you're going.

▶ Go to the interview alone. Don't bring friends, children or relatives to hang around in the waiting room.

▶ You may be asked to fill out a job application form. Take a resume with you, and copy the information to the job application. Give your resume to the interviewer.

▶ When you arrive for the interview, introduce yourself to the receptionist and say that you are scheduled for a job interview with Mr./Ms./Mrs. ___. State the job you are applying for, and the time of your interview. If you don't know the interviewer's name, ask.

Always be extra nice to the receptionist, because the interviewer may ask the receptionist for an opinion of you.

▶ When you are introduced to the interviewer, shake hands firmly, and look the interviewer in the eye. Be enthusiastic and positive, but businesslike. Many job applicants are rejected because they give a limp handshake, and fail to make eye contact!

▶ When you meet the interviewer, find something casual to comment about: the person who referred you, plants or paintings in the employer's office. Try to break the ice and make yourself and the employer comfortable.

▶ Everyone is a little nervous during the interview – including the employer who's asking the questions. A little nervousness is good. It makes you concentrate. Tell yourself to relax a bit and focus on making a good impression. Remember, you're an actor, and this is your role. So play the role, just as you rehearsed it!

When you get to the interview

▶ Bring your resume
▶ Bring a list of all previous employers
▶ Bring references or recommendation letters
▶ Bring your Social Security card and driver's license
▶ Non-citizens should bring an alien registration card
▶ Don't chew gum
▶ Don't smoke

Looks aren't everything – but appearance helps

An employer will probably judge you on his first impression: your appearance.

It can mean the difference between getting hired and not getting hired. You get only one chance to make a good, first impression. If you go to a job interview carelessly groomed, you've lost your chance before you've presented your qualifications to the employer.

Ask yourself this question: Are you willing to change your appearance for about an hour to impress an employer?

How to dress for a job interview in Hawaii

▶ Dress for the next higher position than the one you're applying for
▶ Some people believe men make a better impression wearing a tie, while others believe it's appropriate to wear a nice aloha shirt
▶ Use common sense and simple, good taste in clothes and make-up when you go to a job interview
▶ Look clean and neat. Pay attention to personal hygiene.
▶ Shine your shoes
▶ Clean, comfortable, conservative clothes are your best bet. Don't wear flashy clothes, dangling jewelry, excessive make-up, or heavy fragrance. A "far out" or extreme fashion appearance may hurt your chances for getting a job.
▶ Don't wear sunglasses or a hat when speaking to an employer
▶ Cover your tattoos
▶ Men should avoid wearing jewelry, including earrings

How to act during the job interview

▶ Always sit straight in the chair with your hands folded in your lap. Don't lean back, slouch or appear casual. This is a business interview, not a social chat.

 JOB TIP   If the person interviewing you is very friendly and you feel relaxed, don't fall into the trap of relaxing in your chair. Always act businesslike.

▶ Look directly at the interviewer. Your eyes shouldn't wander around the room.

▶ Think before you answer every question.

▶ Give short answers. Be brief, simple, and to the point.

▶ Show your bright side. Smile and be cheerful, polite, enthusiastic and friendly. People want to hire cheerful people!

▶ If some questions are similar, add new information to each answer, or expand on a previous answer with a specific example of your skills, accomplishments, and experience.

▶ When an employer has many people to interview, he may be rushed to limit the time for each interview. You will make some employers angry if you go overtime.

▶ If some of the employer's questions appear to be irrelevant to the job, it is because the employer wants to know how you present yourself — how you think, talk and act under stress. Stay calm and answer every question patiently and thoughtfully.

▶ Listen carefully when the interviewer talks. Your answers should stick to the subject. Don't ramble.

▶ A few times during the interview, address the interviewer by last name (not first name).

▶ Take the opportunity to stress your strong points. Give examples of your skills and accomplishments in your answers. This is where practice interviewing pays off!

▶ If asked about your weaknesses or dislikes, say something general that turns a negative into a positive.

► Stick to "good work ethic" answers: Tell the interviewer you are dependable, reliable, on time, honest, capable of meeting deadlines, etc. You are a self-starter, a team worker and a quick learner. You will be an asset for the company. Sounds like the Boy Scout code, doesn't it?

► If you lack job experience, emphasize something positive. Tell the interviewer that you get along well with co-workers, you are organized, motivated, dependable, and a fast learner.

► Whenever you can, give an answer with a brief anecdote about an accomplishment or something that reveals you are a fast learner...and a doer.

► At the end of the interview, tell the employer you are interested in the job, and explain why you are qualified.

What to avoid during the job interview

► Never relax too much or let down your guard to a job interviewer who appears to be likable and sympathetic. Retain your businesslike demeanor – hands folded in your lap.

► Don't tell the interviewer, "The information is on my resume."

► Don't reveal any weaknesses about your abilities or anything you disliked about a previous job.

► Don't volunteer any negative information about yourself.

► Don't ever criticize your former boss or co-workers. This would be a **big mistake.** Prospective employers won't hire anyone who criticizes a former boss, no matter how much the criticism is deserving.

▶ Don't say you are desperate for a job, you need the money, you've been turned down for other jobs, or you've been looking for six months. Employers don't want to hire someone who has had difficulty finding a job. Never say "I'll take anything." Make the employer think you are special.

▶ Don't discuss any personal or financial problems. Answer all questions as they relate to the job.

▶ Don't apologize for any lack of experience, education or training. Stress your strong points — such as your accomplishments, ability to learn quickly, assume responsibility, etc.

▶ Don't argue with the interviewer.

▶ Don't talk about salary, vacation, holidays, benefits, etc. until you are offered the job. If you are asked what kind of salary you expect, you might ask what the company is willing to pay for a person with your experience and skills. If the salary is lower than you expected, don't show disappointment. In a positive tone, say you are interested in this job as a career opportunity and you are flexible about the salary.

How to make a terrific impression at the job interview

Congratulations. You've been invited to the job interview. You've been preparing for this moment, so here's your chance to shine.

When answering questions, don't constantly emphasize "I...I...I...." Think about what the company's needs are, what you can do for the employer, and what kind of person the interviewer wants to hire.

Don't take every question literally. The employer may be looking for:

▶ A savvy "gut reaction"

– or –

▶ A slip of your tongue which reveals something you didn't expect to say.

The employer is also looking for answers that display traits such as confidence, enthusiasm, loyalty, and discretion.

The 22 Most Common Interview Questions... and Suggested Answers

"Tell me something about yourself?"

Don't take this question literally. The employer doesn't want you to talk about your family, hobbies or other personal matters. Emphasize why your skills, training, education, experience, and accomplishments would make you good for the company.

Examples:

▶ "I look forward to using my skills here because..."
▶ "I am a self-starter and a results-oriented person. I like to work with people..."

"Why should I hire you?"

The employer has many qualified applicants to interview. How you answer this question may separate you from the pack.

Say something humble, such as: "I know you probably have many other qualified people to interview, however I believe I can do the job because..." Then explain how your skills, training and accomplishments would make you an asset to the company.

"Tell me what you know about our company?"
– or –
"Why do you want to work for our company?"

The employer wants to find out if you've done your homework and learned anything about the company. Never say you know nothing about the company.

If you know very little, then say, "I know that your company is considered a good place to work. You have an excellent reputation for quality products, and high employee morale..."

Explain how your accomplishments or skills fit with the company's goals, policies or accomplishments, or how you can make the company more productive.

Examples:

▶ If you've researched the company, say: "This is a good company because..." (Say something nice about the company, its image, accomplishments, products or services. If you do business with this company or if you like the products, say so.)

▶ "I see good potential for having a long-term career here. You have an excellent reputation for high employee morale, and you offer your employees promotional career opportunities..."

▶ "This office is closer to my home, and a job here would shorten my commute time..."

▶ If you say, "I need a job," you won't get the job. Always express confidence to employers.

"Why do you feel qualified for this job?"

Examples:

▶ "I am a good carpenter with three years of accident-free work."

▶ "I have been a secretary my entire career. I can operate (name the office equipment or computer software you use)..."

"Tell me about your last job?"
– or –
"What didn't you like about your last job?"

The employer may be testing your loyalty and character. Don't complain about your former boss, co-workers, or any specific task you hated doing. Pick a generality and turn it into something positive.

Examples:

- ▶ "I spent an hour driving to work each way. I want to work closer to home."
- ▶ "I had to work a lot of overtime to help my co-workers catch up."
- ▶ "The work wasn't challenging my potential."

"Why did you leave your last job?"

Many people squirm in their chair when they get this question, and it's obvious to the interviewer. Are you worried that you don't have a reasonable explanation to justify why you left your last job? The most common reasons why people leave their jobs may be explained by the acronym **LOSS**:

Location: "The commute time was too long, and I wanted to work closer to home."

Opportunity: "I advanced as far as I could go. There were no career or promotional opportunities available to me."

Salary: "I was underpaid for my skills, experience and knowledge. I wanted better benefits."

Stability: "The company wasn't financially stable. The business closed down...(or) suffered from layoffs and budget cuts."

The interviewer wants to avoid hiring people who are:

- ▶ Job hopping
- ▶ Taking unnecessary sick leave

- ▶ Frequently late
- ▶ Have a bad attitude
- ▶ Can't perform the job
- ▶ Have personal problems

Employers are looking for workers who are loyal and easy to get along with. No matter what happened at your last job, don't speak badly about anyone or anything. Answer the question calmly. It really helps if you've rehearsed your answer.

Don't say you were fired, asked to resign, were unhappy with your job, or involved in any personality conflicts. If you were laid off, you should give an honest answer and say that the company closed down, or cut its payroll and personnel, and many people were let go — including you.

If there is a problem, wait until the employer offers you a job, then mention it if you are asked, or if you feel you must.

Examples:

- ▶ If you were fired or asked to resign:

"I left on a mutual agreement." If you are asked why — turn it around and say something positive.

- ▶ If you had problems such as transportation, child care, illness or other personal matters:

"I lost my job due to a ___ problem. This is no longer a problem."

"What are your strengths and weaknesses?"

Be prepared for this irrelevant question. Mention a general weakness that can be easily turned into a strength. Or explain how you overcame a weakness that you once had. Give the employer a "safe" answer he will appreciate.

Examples of weaknesses:

► "I am very concerned with quality, so I work very hard until I finish the job..."
► "I can't stand to leave a job unfinished, even if I have to stay late..."
► "I am concerned about getting the details right..."
► "I like to be punctual, and am always one of the first to arrive for meetings and appointments."
► "I don't like to discard anything that might be important sometime in the future. I tend to save things, and this often saves the day when someone is looking for a document that other people wanted to throw away."

Examples of strengths:

► "I work well with people..."
► "I am proud of my work accuracy..."
► "I always arrive at work on time..."
► "I can meet deadlines..."
► "I am accurate and creative..."

"What would you do if..."

This is a problem-solving question. Think before you speak. If you want to "buy time" to think, ask for clarification or for more information. You can't be expected to know all the facts and circumstances that apply here. If you've encountered a similar experience, say so, and explain how you may have handled a similar situation.

The employer really wants to know how you would tackle a problem, and if you would consult with others before making a decision. Say: "Naturally, I would research the matter by reading reports that have been written, and I would ask staff and management for their input and advice. Then, once I obtained all possible information from all possible sources, one of the solutions I **might** consider using is..."

"Have you had any serious illnesses or injuries?"

It is illegal for an employer to ask if you've ever received Workers' Compensation, but this question is phrased in a way that is legal. If the answer is no, then there is no problem. If the answer is "yes," have a prepared answer ready, plus a signed statement from your doctor confirming your recovery and your ability to do the job.

"Why have you had so many jobs?"

Examples:

▶ "I wanted to gain experience in many different jobs so I would know what I do well, and what I like best...I've also learned how to handle assignments in different ways..."
▶ "I was affected by unexpected layoffs at my last two jobs. I thought they were stable companies, but they suffered from the economic recession."
▶ "I worked part-time while raising a family. Now that my children are grown, I'm available to work full-time and enter the career I've always wanted."
▶ "Several jobs were part-time while I was in school."

"Aren't you overqualified for this job?"

The employer may be questioning your age, experience, salary expectations or job stability.
Examples:

► "I am a productive worker, and I look forward to moving up the career ladder with your company."
► "I admire your company for its solid reputation. It is well-known as a great place to work and I'd like to advance my career here."
► "I'd like to grow with your company. I don't mind taking a lower paying job because I see a good future here where I can demonstrate my skills and advance..."

"Why should I hire you? You don't have as much experience as other candidates."

Give examples which support your experience in other fields, or give examples of character traits such as:

► "I always meet deadlines..."
► "I am a fast learner..."
► "I work well under pressure..."
► "I get along well with my co-workers..."

"Why have you been unemployed so long?"

This question gives you an opportunity to explain gaps in your employment history. Be careful about explaining illnesses, Workers' Compensation injuries, weak job history, etc.
Examples:

► "Good jobs are hard to find, especially with an excellent and stable company such as yours. I didn't want to take any job

that was offered to me. I prefer to wait for the right job op-portunity with a good company like yours."
▶ "I wasn't unemployed. I pursued my ___ hobby that I developed into a small business..."
▶ "I wasn't unemployed. I took some classes at school to learn new skills that would qualify me for a job at your company..."

"How did you get along with your co-workers?"

Never say anything negative about your previous co-workers.

"My supervisor complimented me on how well I got along with my co-workers..."

Have you ever been a supervisor?

If it is true, say yes, and credit your accomplishments to the support you received from your workers.
If not, say:

"I didn't have the authority to hire or fire anyone, but I coordinated several important projects..."

"What kind of recommendation will your former employer give you?"

It always makes a good impression to show your interviewer a copy of recommendation letters from your former employers, then say something like:

▶ "My former boss will tell you that I got along with my co-workers."
▶ "My former boss will tell you that I did my job well."
▶ "My former boss will tell you that I always came to work on time and was very good at meeting deadlines."

"Do you have references?"

You should bring to your job interview the names, addresses and phone numbers of at least three people (not relatives) who know your work (former bosses or co-workers), and will serve as references. Most employers do not accept relatives as references.

Before you leave your current job, negotiate with your employer for a reference letter. If necessary, draft a letter that minimizes or ignores any bad feelings. Or ask someone other than your boss for a reference letter. Even if you don't get along with your boss, you can probably find something that you did well that he can state in a letter.

"What do you plan on doing five years from now?"
— or —
"What are your career plans?"

The interviewer really wants to know that you won't quit this job for another job elsewhere. Even if you are considering that option, say: "I am definitely seeking a solid long-term job, and I like this company because you offer promotional opportunities for career advancement."

"What starting salary will you accept?"

Avoid talking about salary, vacation, holidays, benefits, etc. until you are offered the job. If you are asked what kind of salary you expect, you should say you are "open" or "it is negotiable."

If pushed to answer how much salary you expect, ask what the salary range is.

If the employer still insists on knowing how much income you expect, you should say: "Let's discuss salary when I receive a job offer."

If the employer names a salary range that is lower than you expected, don't show disappointment. Be enthusiastic and say: "I am very interested in this job as a career opportunity, and I am flexible about the salary."

Questions you can ask the interviewer

Employers usually give you the opportunity to ask questions. Curiously, many job seekers can't think of any questions to ask. That's because they go to interviews without any knowledge of the company. If you don't ask questions, the employer will think you don't know much about the company, or that you just don't care.

You should ask questions that show a career interest in the company, and in the job you are applying for. Ask a few questions from these examples:

► "What are the typical daily duties of this job?"
► "Please elaborate on the major job duties?"
► "What are the greatest difficulties of the job?"
► "Who will I report to?"
► If you are a supervisor: "Who will report to me?"
► "What kind of job performance review system is used to evaluate employees, and how often?"
► "How does this job relate to other jobs in the office?"
► "How does this job relate to the short-term and long-term goals of the company?"
► "How long has the company had this position?"
► "Why did the last person leave this position?"
► "What is the turnover rate for this job?"
► "Do people work a lot of overtime?"
► "Do you have flexible work hours?"
► "What promotional opportunities are there?"

As the job interview ends

▶ If the employer didn't say when you will be contacted about the selection decision, ask when you can call to find out.

▶ Before you leave, make a "closing statement": ask the interviewer for the job. Yes, ask for the job, in a confident tone of voice. Tell the employer why you want to work for the company. Explain that you admire the company for its accomplishments, products or services. Or say that it's a good company known for treating its employees with respect, offering promotional opportunities, good benefits, etc., and you would enjoy the opportunity to work there.

▶ Give a firm handshake, thank the employer for his time, and for considering you for the job.

▶ Ask the interviewer for a business card.

JOB TIP

By asking for the job, you are expressing a positive interest in the company. It makes you stand out, in an active rather than a passive way.

After the job interview

Immediately after the interview, ask yourself:

- ► Did I talk too much or too little?
- ► Did I explain how my qualifications were relevant to the job?
- ► Did I forget to say something important?
- ► Did I say or do anything that may have interested the employer?
- ► Did I say or do anything that I should not have?
- ► Did I act defensively when answering any questions?
- ► Did I show that I knew enough about the company or the position?
- ► Did I dress appropriately?
- ► Did I ask for the job at the end of the interview?
- ► How can I improve my next job interview?

Send a thank you letter

When you get home, send a letter thanking the employer for the job interview, and expressing your interest in the company. Mail the letter right away.

Why write a "thank you" letter? Sometimes it's the little things that count.

- ► A "thank you" letter makes a good impression. Few people send them, so the employer is more likely to remember you and think highly of your professionalism.

- ► If the employer can't decide between hiring you and another person, and the other person doesn't write a "thank you" letter — you may get the job.

▶ A "thank you" letter gives you an opportunity to clarify any significant point that you want to make.

If you haven't been contacted in two weeks, call the employer. It might give the employer an opportunity to ask more questions, or to clarify something important. Point out that you are interested in the job, you'd like to work for the company, and that your qualifications and skills provide a good match for the position.

Be sure to refer to your job search file when you call, and make notes.

Should I take the job?

Don't be so desperate or blind that you jump at any job opportunity. Many people jump at the first job offer, only to regret their decision later. You end up hating the new job more than the job you just left.

The sophisticated job seeker will try to avoid making a poor decision based solely on a formal interview with a company hiring manager.

Tell the employer you want a few days to think about it.

What you don't know can hurt you — so if you don't know much about the company, do some research now, before it's too late, and find out:

▶ Is it a good place to work?
▶ Are their career opportunities?
▶ Are their job training opportunities?
▶ What is the employee turnover?
▶ Are you expected to work a lot of overtime?
▶ Is the supervisor is a good boss?
▶ What is the company's management style?
▶ Does the company have any serious financial problems?
▶ Are workers concerned about rumors of upcoming layoffs?

Sample thank you letter

Jennifer Sloan
110 Mahalo St.
Honolulu, HI 96825
phone 222-3333

date

Ms. Ellen Tanaka
Beautiful Clothes
1200 Kala St.
Honolulu, HI 96813

Dear _____:

I enjoyed the opportunity to interview for the Sales Associate position. It is exactly the kind of position I am seeking.

Your company has an outstanding reputation for quality clothes and customer service, and I would be honored to join your team. I make this claim, both as a sales professional, and as a loyal customer of your store.

My sales skills and experience, and knowledge of your company, would make me a productive employee right away.

If you need additional information about my skills or experience, please don't hesitate to call me at 222-3333.

Cordially,

Jennifer Sloan

Try to get answers to these and other questions by calling:

► People who work in the office where you'd work
► Other people in the company
► Former employees of that company
► Workers in the same profession at other companies

If you accept the job, congratulations!!! Otherwise, you will be relieved to discover that the job may not be as wonderful as the employer made it appear to be.

If you aren't hired, ask why

Once in a while, call and ask the interviewer for advice so you can do better at future job interviews. Tell the employer that you are calling because you felt very comfortable during the interview and you thought he was sincerely interested in you. This may flatter him.

The employer may offer helpful suggestions. You might learn something important about your level of skills and work experience. Ask if the employer checked your references. If so, ask if they all gave favorable comments.

Ask if the employer can suggest the names of other employers who may need someone with your job skills. It never hurts to ask.

Practice makes perfect

Continue to practice interviewing with a friend who will suggest how you can improve your answers. The more you practice, the better your real job interviews will be.

Keep calling

Stick to your job search plan. Continue tapping the hidden job market by making phone calls, writing letters, obtaining information interviews, seeking referrals, and upgrading your skills.

It's all about PRIDE

Finding a good job is all about pride. Pride keeps you going when the going gets tough. Pride motivates you to keep making those phone calls, setting up appointments, and rehearsing your job interview skills.

Pride is something no one can take away from you – no matter how long it takes you to find the right job.

 JOB TIP   Have pride in yourself, and you will have the self-confidence to succeed, and get the job you want!

Hawaii's 1,600 top companies

Top Oahu Companies

Accountants

Arthur Andersen
737 Bishop St #2900
Honolulu 96813
526-2255

Coopers & Lybrand
999 Bishop #1900
Honolulu 96813
531-3400

Deloitte & Touche LLP
1132 Bishop St #1200
Honolulu 96813
543-0700

Ernst & Young
1001 Bishop Pauahi 2400
Honolulu 96813
531-2037

Grant Thornton
1132 Bishop #1000
Honolulu 96813
536-0066

Ikeda & Wong CPA
1001 Bishop St
Pacific #1717
Honolulu 96813
524-3660

K P M G Peat Marwick
1001 Bishop Pauahi 2100
Honolulu 96813
531-7286

Nishihama & Kishida
CPAs
1001 Bishop Pacific
1760
Honolulu 96813
524-2255

PKF-Hawaii
1100 Alakea St #2100
Honolulu 96813
521-1021

Price Waterhouse LLP
707 Richards St #728
Honolulu 96813
941-7755

Agriculture

Aloha Lei Greeters
Box 29133
Honolulu 96820
951-9990

Akahi Services
99-1076 Iwaena St.
Aiea 96701
488-5995

Del Monte Fresh
Produce Hawaii
94-1000 Kunia Rd
Kunia 96759
621-1208

Dole Fresh Fruit Co -
Hawaii
1116 Whitmore Ave
Wahiawa 96786
621-3200

Green Thumb
3363 Campbell Ave
Honolulu 96815
732-2868

Hawaii Agriculture
Research Center   *No.*
99-193 Aiea Hts #300
Aiea 96701
487-5561

Trees of Hawaii
91-326 Kauhi St *N/o*
Kapolei 96707
682-5771

Automotive
car dealers, retail supplies and equipment, car rental, repair, service stations, etc.

Alamo Rent a Car
3055 N Nimitz Hwy
Honolulu 96819
833-4585

Aloha Petroleum
1132 Bishop St
Honolulu 96813
522-9700

Ampco System Parking
841 Bishop #601
Honolulu 96813
522-1280

Apcoa
1001 Bishop Pauahi 600
Honolulu 96813
531-3128

Automotive Warehouse
2670 Waiwai Lp
Honolulu 96819
836-0331

Avis Rent A Car Systems
2912 Aolele
Honolulu 96819
834-5536

BMW of Honolulu
1075 S Beretania St
Honolulu 96814
536-7052

Budget Rent A Car Hawaii
550 Paiea St #236
Honolulu 96819
838-2221

Charles W Carter Co
1299 Kaumualii
Honolulu 96817
832-6292

Cutter Automotive Team
1311 Kapiolani #200
Honolulu 96814
592-5401

Cutter Dodge Chrysler
Plymouth
735 Dillingham Blvd
Honolulu 96817
842-6300

Cutter Ford/Isuzu
98-015 Kamehameha Hwy
Aiea 96701
487-3811

Cutter Geo/Chevrolet
1391 Kapiolani Blvd
Honolulu 96814
946-8311

Diamond Parking
439 Kamani St
Honolulu 96813
592-7275

Dollar Rent A Car
1600 Kapiolani Blvd #825
Honolulu 96814
926-4242

Enterprise Rent-a-Car
609 Ahua
Honolulu 96819
836-7722

Goodyear Auto Service
Center
2312 Kamehameha Hwy
#A-2
Honolulu 96819
845-1015

Hertz Rent A Car
233 Keawe #625
Honolulu 96813
523-5181

Honda Windward
45-671 Kamehameha
Hwy
Kaneohe 96744
247-8544

Honolulu Ford
711 Ala Moana Blvd
Honolulu 96813
532-1700

J N Automotive Group
2999 N Nimitz Hwy
Honolulu 96819
831-2500

Jobbers Auto Warehouse
Supply
2101 Auiki St
Honolulu 96819
845-6421

Lex Brodie's Tire Co
701 Queen St
Honolulu 96813
536-9381

Midas Muffler Shops
1415 Dillingham
Honolulu 96817
841-7361

Mike McKenna's
Windward Ford
725 Kailua Rd
Kailua 96734
266-7000

Mike McKenna's
Windward Volkswagen
Mazda
105 Oneawa
Kailua 96734
266-8000

Mike Salta Lincoln
Mercury Pontiac Isuzu
2945 N Nimitz Hwy
Honolulu 96819
836-2441

Napa Auto Parts
747 Ilaniwai
Honolulu 96813
592-4344

Napa Distribution
Center-Hawaii
94-141 Leowaena St
Waipahu 96797
671-4081

National Car Rental
3223 N Nimitz Hwy
Honolulu 96819
834-7186

New City Nissan
900 Ala Moana Blvd
Honolulu 96814
524-9111

Nissan Motor Corp in
Hawaii
2880 Kilihau
Honolulu 96819
836-0848

Pacific Mazda Subaru
94-223 Farrington Hwy
Waipahu 96797
671-5115

Pacific Nissan
94-119 Farrington Hwy
Waipahu 96797
671-2611

Pacific Oldsmobile-GMC-
Volkswagen
98-055 Kamehameha Hwy
Aiea 96701
487-5526

Pflueger Acura
1450 S Beretania
Honolulu 96814
942-4555

Pflueger Honda
777 Ala Moana Blvd
Honolulu 96813
528-7200

Propark
445 Seaside Ave #602
Honolulu 96815
971-7755

Ron's Auto Parts &
Performance
2760 Kilihau
Honolulu 96819
831-7667

Saturn of Honolulu
2901 N Nimitz Hwy
Honolulu 96819
836-7007

Schuman Carriage Buick-
Cadillac-Subaru
1234 S Beretania St
Honolulu 96814
592-4500

Service Motors Wahiawa
105 S Kamehameha Hwy
Wahiawa 96786
622-4195

Tony Honda Pearlridge
98-051 Kamehameha Hwy
Aiea 96701
487-5595

Tony Management Group
98-055 Kamehameha Hwy
Aiea 96701
487-5595

Windward Auto Sales
46-177 Kahuhipa
Kaneohe 96744
233-6000

Windward Dodge
46-177 Kahuhipa St
Kaneohe 96744
233-6000

Windward Nissan Olds
GMC
46-151 Kahuhipa
Kaneohe 96744
235-6433

Building cleaners, pest control

All Star/Sab
2865 Pukoloa St
Honolulu, HI 96819
833-8133

Armstrong Building
Maintenance
650 Iwilei
Honolulu 96817
526-0133

Coral Janitorial Service
Box 17640
Honolulu 96817
845-7792

Hawaiian Buuilding
Maintenance Co
412 Keawe St
Honolulu 96813
537-4561

Kleenco Corp
3015 Koapaka St
Honolulu 96819
831-7600

Lion's Cleaning &
Maintenance
846 Pohukaina #C
Honolulu 96813
597-1771

Metropolitan Maintenance
1113 Artesian St
Honolulu 96826
944-8211

No Ka Oi Termite & Pest
96-1272 Waihona
Pearl City 96782
456-4214

Shiny Floors
3312B Campbell Ave
Honolulu 96815
735-9991

Worldwide Services
Box 700579
Kapolei 96707
847-8833

Xtermco
1020 Auahi St
Honolulu 96814
591-2922

Business Services
Advertising and public relations, business consulting, research, employment agencies

Adecco
1001 Bishop Pauahi
2001
Honolulu, HI 96813
533-8889

Adworks
444 Hobron 4th floor
Honolulu, HI 96815
955-4416

Altres
711 Kapiolani #110
Honolulu, HI 96813
591-4900

Attco
2855 Koapaka St
Honolulu 96819
836-1191

Cardinal Services
552 N Nimitz
Honolulu, HI 96817
538-3884

Communications
Pacific
820 Mililani #400
Honolulu 96813
521-5391

DHL Worldwide Express
3375 Koapaka St
Honolulu 96819
836-0441

Ebb Tides
1854A Mahana
Honolulu 96816
734-5055

Employee Management
Corp
711 Kapiolani Blvd
Honolulu 96813
591-4990

GTE Directories Corp
711 Kapiolani Blvd
Honolulu 96813
593-8300

Interim Personnel
1441 Kapiolani St #1212
Honolulu 96814
942-2333

JS Services
1314 S King St #1163
Honolulu 96814
596-2727

Kalama Services
3049 Ualena St #101
Honolulu 96819
836-0050

Kokua Nurses and Para
Professionals
1210 Auahi St #223
Honolulu 96814
536-2326

Labor Services
711 Kapiolani Blvd
Honolulu 96813
591-4950

McNeil Wilson Communi-
cations
1001 Bishop Pauahi #950
Honolulu 96813
531-0244

Milici Valenti Ng Pack
Advertising
999 Bishop St #2400
Honolulu 96813
536-0881

Nursefinders
1100 Ward Ave #700
Honolulu 96814
522-6050

Olsten Staffing Services
900 Fort Street #1202
Honolulu 96813
523-3313

Omnitrak Group
841 Bishop #725
Honolulu 96813
528-4050

RGIS Inventory Specialists
1860 Ala Moana Blvd
#407B
Honolulu 96815
941-2282

SMS Research
1042 Fort Street Mall
#200
Honolulu 96813
537-3356

Starr Seigle McCombs
1001 Bishop Pacific #1900
Honolulu 96813
524-5080

Uni-Check
111 N Kng St #501
Honolulu 96817
524-2030

Washington Inventory
Service
99-061 Koaha Way #205
Aiea 96701
486-7885

Computer
data processing, equipment, retail sales

Ceridian Employer
Services
2828 Paa #1010
Honolulu 96819
837-2200

Comp U S A
500 Ala Moana Blvd
#210
Honolulu 96813
537-1355

Computer City
94-875 Lumiaina St
Waipahu 96797
676-3200

Data House
1585 Kapiolani Blvd
Honolulu 96814
942-8108

I B M Corp
1240 Ala Moana
Honolulu 96814
597-9555

Interisland Systems
Development & Integration
1600 Kapiolani #1100
Honolulu HI 96814
944-8742

Kapiolani InfoServices
1946 Young St #300
Honolulu 96826
973-7000

Kapiolani Info Services
55 Merchant St #2300
Honolulu 96826
535-7177

Liberty House Information
Service
420 Waiakamilo Rd #416
Honolulu 96817
945-8400

Square USA
55 Merchant #3100
Honolulu 96813
535-9000

Uniden
1132 Bishop 24th floor
Honolulu 96813
535-1800

Unisys Corp
711 Kapiolani #425
Honolulu 96813
591-7000

Verifone
100 Kahelu Ave
Mililani 96789
623-2911

Contractors

Alcal Hawaii
91-446 Komohana St
#A
Kapolei 96707
682-5222

A-1 A-Lectrician
2849 Kaihikapu St
Honolulu 96819
839-2771

Air Engineering Co
2308 Pahounui Dr
Honolulu 96819
848-1040

Alaka'i Mechanical
Corporation
2655 Waiwai Loop
Honolulu 96819
834-1085

Albert C Kobayashi
94-535 Ukee St
Waipahu 96797
671-6460

Alert Alarm of Hawaii
1270 Queen Emma St
Honolulu 96813
528-6423

Alii Glass & Metal
94-144 Leoole St
Waipahu 96797
671-4571

Allied Builders System
1717 Akahi St
Honolulu 96819
847-3763

Allied Construction
1917 Homerule
Honolulu 96819
841-0177

Aloha Painting Co
99-1350 Koaha Pl
Aiea 96701
483-3232

Amelco
2308 Pahounui Dr
Honolulu 96819
845-9324

American Electric Co
2308 Pahounui Dr
Honolulu 96819
848-0751

American Tradition Homes
98-1268 Kaahumanu St
#C3
Pearl City 96782
627-0733

Associated Steelworkers
91-156 Kalaeloa
Kapolei 96707
682-5588

Bodell Construction
56-701 Kamehameha Hwy
Kahuku 96731
293-0609

Close Electric
759 Puuloa Rd
Honolulu 96819
833-2702

Coastal Construction Co
1900 Hau St
Honolulu 96819
847-3277

Constructors Hawaii
740 Kohou
Honolulu 96817
848-2455

Continental Mechanical of
the Pacific
2146 Puuhale Pl
Honolulu 96819
845-5936

Delta Construction Corp
91-255 Oihana St
Kapolei 96707
682-1315

Dillingham Construction
Pacific
614 Kapahulu Ave
Honolulu 96815
735-3211

Dover Elevator Company
1268 Young St #300
Honolulu 96814
955-6638

Dura/Constructors
1210D N. Nimitz Hwy
Honolulu 96817
521-9499

E & E Masonry
1654 Kaumoli
Pearl City 96782
455-3440

Electricians Hawaii
96-1382 Waihona St #6
Pearl City 96782
456-5941

Finance Homebuilders
92-555 Makakilo Dr
Kapolei 96707
672-3577

Fletcher Pacific Construction Co
707 Richards St #400
Honolulu 96813
533-5000

Fujikawa Thomas
Painting Co
2865 Ualena
Honolulu 96819
836-2011

Glover, Jas W
725 Kapiolani #326
Honolulu 96813
591-8977

Grace Pacific Corp
99-1300 Halawa Valley
Aiea 96701
487-7916

Group Builders
2020 Democrat St
Honolulu 96819
832-0888

Haitsuka Brothers
Trucking
50 Sand Island Access
Road
Honolulu 96819
847-0631

Hawaiian Bitumuls &
Paving
110 Puuhale Rd
Honolulu 96819
845-3991

Hawaiian Dredging
Construction Co
614 Kapahulu Ave
Honolulu 96815
735-3211

Heide & Cook
1714 Kanakanui St
Honolulu 96819
841-6161

Highway Construction
Co
720 Umi St
Honolulu 96819
841-5511

Honolulu Painting Co
2809 Mokumoa St
Honolulu 96819
839-2777

Ideal Construction
1038 Ulupono St
Honolulu 96819
848-0502

Industrial Welding
3169 Ualena St
Honolulu 96819
836-1776

Inouye, Ralph S Co
2831 Awaawaloa
Honolulu 96819
839-9002

Jade Painting & Decorat-
ing
99-1066 Iwaena St
Aiea 96701
487-0025

Key Construction
50 Sand Island Access Rd
Honolulu 96819
842-3174

Kiewit Pacific Co
1001 Kamokila #305
Kapolei 96707
674-1088

Koga Engineering &
Construction
1162 Mikole
Honolulu 96819
845-7829

Lee, R H S
96-1414 Waihona Pl
Pearl City 96782
455-9026

Morrison Knudsen Corp
91-252 Kuhela St
Kapolei 96707
682-2085

Mortenson Construction
1099 Alakea St #1580
Honolulu 96813
524-0086

Murphy, G W Construc-
tion Co
650 Kakoi St
Honolulu 96819
836-0454

Mutual Welding Co
739 Ahua
Honolulu 96819
839-5111

Oahu Air Conditioning
Service
938 Kohou
Honolulu 96817
848-0156

Oahu Construction Co
3375 Koapaka #H490
Honolulu 96819
836-2981

Oahu Painting &
Decorating
99-139 Waiua Way #A
Aiea 96701
486-8171

Okada Trucking Co
2065 S King St #105
Honolulu 96826
946-4894

Ono Construction
747 Amana St #220
Honolulu 96814
942-9465

Otis Elevator Co
793 S Hotel
Honolulu 96813
599-1111

Pacific Isle Pool Distributors
201 Kapaa Quarry Rd
Kailua 96734
261-0822

Paul's Electrical Service
45-552 Kamehameha Hwy
Kaneohe 96744
247-2464

Pioneer Contracting Co
930 Kilani Ave
Wahiawa 96786
622-4161

Quality General
99-1245 Waiua Pl
Aiea 96701
487-3614

R W C Hawaii
2621 Waiwai Lp
Honolulu 96819
836-2854

Ralph S Inouye Co
2831 Awaawaloa St #201
Honolulu 96819
839-9002

Ray Higdon Construction
91-255 Kalaeloa Blvd
Kapolei 96707
682-7188

Reef Development of
Hawaii
99-930 Iwaena #107B
Aiea 96701
488-1228

Robert M Kaya Builders
525 Kokea St Bldg B-3
Honolulu 96817
845-6477

Royal Contracting Co
677 Ahua St
Honolulu 96819
839-9006

S & M Sakamoto
96-1385 Waihona St
Pearl City 96782
456-4717

S & M Welding Co
1024 Puuwai St
Honolulu 96819
848-0090

Site Engineering
545 Kaaahi St
Honolulu 96817
841-8883

Society Painters
96-1403 Waihona Pl
Pearl City 96782
455-8157

Steel Tech
99-1379 Koaha Pl
Aiea 96701
487-1445

Sun Industries
660 Mapunapuna St
Honolulu 96819
833-2502

Tower Construction
2829 Awaawaloa #200
Honolulu 96819
839-1942

U S Pacific Builders Inc
1001 Bishop St #1250
Honolulu 96813
523-8554

W E Painting
94-416 Ukee St
Waipahu 96797
671-6785

Walker Moody
Construction Co
2927 Mokumoa St
Honolulu 96819
839-2781

Wasa Electrical Service
2908 Kaihikapu St
Honolulu 96819
839-2741

Wayne's Carpet
3025 Waialae Ave
Honolulu 96816
735-3005

Western Engineering
94-285 Pupuole St
Waipahu 96797
671-6715

Zelinsky D & Sons of
Hawaii
91-310 Komohana St
Kapolei 96707
682-1321

Construction, building equipment and sales
retail, wholesale and distribution

Allied Machinery Corp
94-168 Leoole
Waipahu 96797
671-0541

American Fence
Corporation
96-1373 Waihona St
Pearl City 96782
455-6591

American Machinery
91-291 Kalaeloa #B12
Kapolei 96707
682-0447

Bacon Universal Co
91-3110 hanua St
Kapolei 96707
682-0900

Bonded Materials Co
91-400 Komohana
Kapolei 96707
673-2000

City Mill
46-209 Kahuhipa
Kaneohe 96744
247-8181

City Mill
94-157 Leoleo
Waipahu 96797
671-1746

City Mill
333 Keahole
Honolulu 96825
396-5151

City Mill
3086 Waialae
Honolulu 96816
735-7636

City Mill Co
660 N Nimitz Hwy
Honolulu 96817
533-3811

City Mill Company
95-455 Makaimoimo St
Mililani 96789
623-3100

City Mill Company
98-1277 Kaahumanu St
Aiea 96701
487-3636

Eagle Hardware
94-805 Lumiaina St
Waipahu 96797
676-8381

FKS Rentals & Sales
663 Kakoi
Honolulu 96819
836-2961

G E Supply Hawaii
2312 Kamehameha Hwy
Honolulu 96819
852-6800

Hawaii Pipe & Supply
801 Moowaa St
Honolulu 96817
832-7473

Honsador Lumber
Corporation
91-151 Malakole St
Kapolei 96707
682-2011

Jorgensen Steel &
Aluminum
91-104 Kalaeloa Blvd
Kapolei 96707
682-2020

Kilgo's
180 Sand Island Access Rd
Honolulu 96819
832-2200

Midpac Lumber Co
1001 Ahua
Honolulu 96819
836-8111

Pacific Machinery
94-025 Farrington Hwy
Waipahu 96797
676-0223

Plumbing Specialties &
Supplies
925 Kokea St
Honolulu 96817
841-8711

R S I - Roofing Supply
1081 Makepono
Honolulu 96819
847-2077

Theo H Davies & Co
810 Kapiolani
Honolulu 96813
592-3900

Trane Pacific Service
330 Sand Island Access Rd
Honolulu 96819
845-6662

True Value Hardware
46-184 Kahuhipa St
Kaneohe 96744
235-6623

Wesco Distribution
1030 Mapunapuna
Honolulu 96819
839-7261

Detective, security

Alert Alarm of Hawaii
1270 Queen Emma St
Honolulu 96813
528-6423

Burns International
Security Services
401 Waiakamilo Rd #202
Honolulu 96817
842-4800

Centurion Security
Systems
630 Puuloa Rd
Honolulu 96819
833-6631

Diebold
3375 Koapaka #B-270
Honolulu 96819
837-6400

Engineered Security
Specialist
1270 Queen Emma St
Honolulu 96813
528-6401

Freeman Guards
1130 N Nimitz Hwy 226
Honolulu 96817
532-2944

Hawaii Protective
Association
1290A Maunakea St
Honolulu 96817
537-5938

Honolulu Merchant Patrol
& Guard Co
99-1036 Iwaena St
Aiea 96701
487-9955

International Total
Services
300 Rodgers
Honolulu 96819
839-8046

Loomis Fargo
1540 Kalani St
Honolulu 96817
841-7511

Pacific Knight Security
Box 935
Pearl City 96782
456-8811

Royal Guard Security
1251 S King St #F
Honolulu 96814
596-0848

Royal Guard Security
94-216 Farrington Hwy
Waipahu 96797
676-4409

Safeguard Services
1000 Bishop #608
Honolulu 96813
526-2002

Security Armored Car
and Courrier Service
Box 2073
Honolulu 96805
845-5471

Sentinel Silent Alarm
Co
99-1036 Iwaena St
Aiea 96701
487-0088

Star Protection Agency
707 Richards St #PH-6
Honolulu 96813
532-3911

Wackenhut Corporation
3375 Koapaka #D-105
Honolulu, HI 96819
839-1185

WMP Security Service
Company
94-801 Farrington Hwy
3204
Kapolei 96707
678-9800

Diversified conglomerates, parent companies

Alexander & Baldwin
822 Bishop
Honolulu 96813
525-6611

Amfac/JMB Hawaii
700 Bishop St #2002
Honolulu, HI 96813
543-8900

Bishop Estate
567 S King
Honolulu 96813
523-6200

C S Wo & Sons
4360 Malaai
Honolulu 96818
423-0008

Castle & Cooke
650 Iwilei Rd
Honolulu 96817
548-4811

Chun Kim Chow
Box 1578
Honolulu 96806
532-5725

Daiei
801 Kaheka St
Honolulu 96814
973-4800

Dillingham Construction
Pacific
614 Kapahulu Ave
Honolulu 96815
735-3211

Dole Food Company
1116 Whitmore Ave
Wahiawa 96786
621-3200

Gentry Comanies
Box 295
Honolulu 96809
599-8200

HTH
140 Liliuuokalani #300
Honolulu 96815
923-1595

Hawaiian Electric
Industries
900 Richards St
Honolulu 96813
543-5662

Horita, Herbert K Realty
2024 N King
Honolulu 96819
847-4241

Kyo-Ya Co
2255 Kalakaua Ave #200
Honolulu 96815
931-8600

Pacific Marine & Supply
841 Bishop #1880
Honolulu 96813
531-7001

Pleasant Hawaiian
Holidays
2222 Kalakaua Ave 16th
floor
Honolulu 96815
926-1833

Ralston Enterprises
99-969 Iwaena St
Aiea 96701
487-9919

Roberts Hawaii
680 Iwilei Rd #700
Honolulu 96817
523-7750

Sen Plex Corp
904 Kohou St
Honolulu 96817
848-0111

Servco Pacific
900 Fort St Mall #600
Honolulu 96813
521-6511

Shinwa Golf Hawaii Co
2255 Kuhio #1600
Honolulu 96815
926-1407

Standard Capital Group
705 S King St #204
Honolulu 96813
531-6515

Sultan Company
3049 Ualena St #1400
Honolulu 96819
923-4971

Tesoro Hawaii Petroleum
733 Bishop St #2700
Honolulu 96813
547-3111

Theo H Davies & Co
810 Kapiolani
Honolulu 96813
592-3900

Waterhouse Properties
670 Queen St #200
Honolulu 96813
592-4800

Watumull Brothers
307 Lewers #600
Honolulu 96815
971-8800

Electric, gas, oil, sanitation

AES Hawaii
91-086 Kaomi Loop
Kapolei 96707
682-5330

B F I-Browning Ferris
Indusustries
91-310 Hanua St
Kapolei 96707
682-0900

BFI Waste Systems
207 Puuhale Rd
Honolulu 96819
842-3189

Chevron USA/Refinery
91-480 Malakole St
Kapolei 96707
682-5711

East Honolulu Community
Services
8480 Kalanianaole Hwy
#300
Honolulu 96825
397-3427

Gas Co, The
515 Kamakee
Honolulu 96814
535-5900

Gaspro
2305 Kamehameha Hwy
Honolulu 96819
842-2201

Hawaiian Electric
Company
900 Richards St
Honolulu 96813
543-7771

Honolulu Disposal Service
Box 30968
Honolulu 96820
845-7581

Honolulu Resource
Recovery Venture
91-174 Hanua
Kapolei 96707
682-2099

HRRV
91-174 Hanua St
Kapolei 96707
673-7330

Philip Services Corp
91-127 Malakole St
Kapolei 96707
682-3033

Reynolds Aluminum
Recycling
99-1160 Iwaena
Aiea 96701
487-2802

Tesoro Hawaii Petroleum
Corp
733 Bishop St #2700
Honolulu 96813
547-3111

Engineers, architects

AM Partners
1164 Bishop St #1000
Honolulu 96813
526-2828

Architects Hawaii
1001 Bishop Pacific
#300
Honolulu 96813
523-9636

Austin Tsutsumi &
Associates
501 Sumner #521
Honolulu 96817
533-3646

Belt Collins Hawaii
680 Ala Moana Blvd
1st floor
Honolulu 96813
521-5361

Engineer Surveyors
Hawaii
1020 Auahi St Bldg 6
Honolulu 96814
591-8116

G M P Associates
841 Bishop St #1501
Honolulu 96813
521-4711

G T E Systems
Government Services
3049 Ualena #901
Honolulu 96819
833-0004

G Y A Architects
1357 Kapiolani #1230
Honolulu 96814
955-3009

Geolabs Hawaii
2006 Kalihi St
Honolulu 96819
841-5064

Group 70 International
925 Bethel St 5th floor
Honolulu 96813
523-5866

Kajioka Okada Yamachi
Architects
934 Pumehana St
Honolulu 96826
949-7770

Kober/Hansssen/
Mitchell Architects
55 Merchant St #1400
Honolulu 96813
566-0122

M & E Pacific
1001 Bishop St
Honolulu 96813
521-3051

Oceanit Laboratories
1100 Alakea St 31st fl
Honolulu 96813
531-3017

Okamoto Wilson and
Associates
1907 S Beretania 4th
floor
Honolulu 96826
946-2277

Park Engineering
567 S King St #300
Honolulu 96813
531-1676

Parsons Brinckerhoff
Quade & Douglas
1001 Bishop St Pacific
#3000
Honolulu 96813
531-7094

R M Towill Corporation
420 Waiakamilo Rd
#411
Honolulu, HI 96817
842-1133

Raytheon Services
Pacific
965 N Nimitz Hwy #A4
Honolulu 96817
521-0902

SSFM Engineers
501 Sumner St #502
Honolulu 96817
531-1308

Wimberly Allison Tong
& Goo
700 Bishop St #1800
Honolulu, HI 96813
521-8888

Financial institutions, credit unions,
stock brokers, investments

American Express
Financial Advisors
1585 Kapiolani Blvd
Honolulu 96814
942-7797

American Savings Bank
915 Fort St Mall
Honolulu 96813
531-6262

Associates Financial
Services
98-751 Kuahao Pl #200
Pearl City 96782
486-8681

Bank of Hawaii
111 S King
Honolulu 96813
643-3888

Bank of Honolulu
841 Bishop
Honolulu 96813
543-3700

Central Pacific Bank
220 S King
Honolulu 96813
544-0500

City Bank
201 Merchant St
Honolulu 96813
535-2595

Commercial Credit Corp
700 Bishop St
Honolulu 96813
531-7215

Dean Witter Reynolds
1001 Bishop Pacific
#1600
Honolulu 96813
525-6900

E A Buck Co
55 Merchant #1880
Honolulu 96813
545-2211

Finance Enterprises
1164 Bishop St
Honolulu 96813
548-3311

Finance Factors
1164 Bishop
Honolulu 96813
548-4940

First Federal S & L
Association
851 Fort St
Honolulu, HI 96813
531-9411

First Hawaiian Bank
999 Bishop
Honolulu 96813
525-7000

G T E Hawaiian Tel
Employees FCU
1138 N King
Honolulu 96817
832-8700

GE Capital Hawaii
745 Fort St Mall 18th
floor
Honolulu 96813
527-8200

Hawaii Central Credit
Union
681 S King St
Honolulu 96813
531-8911

Hawaii National Bank
45 N King
Honolulu 96817
528-7711

Hawaii State Employees
FCU
560 Halekauwila St
Honolulu 96813
536-7717

Hickam FCU
40 Hickam Ct
Honolulu 96818
423-1391

Honolulu City Employees
FCU
832 S Hotel St
Honolulu 96813
531-3711

Honolulu Federal
Employees FCU
300 Ala Moana Blvd
Honolulu 96813
523-7037

Honolulu Mortgage
Company
201 Merchant #1700
Honolulu 96813
544-3400

International Savings &
Loan Association
201 Merchant St
Honolulu 96813
535-2700

Island Community
Lending
201 Merchant #2120
Honolulu 96813
545-1000

Merrill Lynch
1001 Bishop St Pauahi PH
Honolulu 96813
525-7300

National Mortgage &
Finance Co
1022 Bethel
Honolulu 96813
531-1311

North American Mortgage
Co
1001 Bishop Pacific 2400
Honolulu 96813
521-8505

Oahu Educational
Employees FCU
1226 College Walk
Honolulu 96817
534-4345

Pacific Century Financial
Corp
Box 2900
Honolulu 96846
643-3888

Pacific Century Trust
111 S King St
Honolulu 96813
538-4444

Pearl Harbor FCU
295 7th St
Honolulu 96818
423-1331

Prudential Securities
500 Ala Moana #2-400
Honolulu 96813
547-5200

Smith Barney
1099 Alakea St FL 23
Honolulu 96813
521-2961

Territorial Savings &
Loan Association
1440 Kapiolani 14th
floor
Honolulu 96814
946-1400

University of Hawaii
FCU
2010 East West Rd
Honolulu 96822
983-5500

Food and beverage
retail, wholesale and distribution, grocers, etc.

7-Eleven Hawaii
1755 Nuuanu Ave #200
Honolulu 96817
526-1711

99 Ranch Market
1151 Mapunapuna St
Honolulu 96819
833-8899

ABC Store
766 Pohukaina
Honolulu 96813
591-2550

Aloha Maid Juice Co
125 Puuhale Rd
Honolulu 96819
847-4477

Anheuser-Bush
99-877 Iwaena
Aiea 96701
487-0055

Armstrong Produce
651 Ilalo St Bldg A
Honolulu 96813
538-7051

Bakery Europa
500 Alakawa St #120
Honolulu 96817
845-5011

Better Brands
94-501 Kau St
Waipahu 96797-4236
676-6111

Big Way Super Markets
94-340 Waipahu Depot
Waipahu 96797
677-3171

C & F Cereal & Fruit
Products
94-501 Kau
Waipahu 96797
676-6166

Cookie Masters of Hawaii
1154 Fort Street #417
Honolulu 96813
537-9278

Daiei
801 Kaheka St
Honolulu 96814
973-4800

Down To Earth Natural
Foods
2525 S King St
Honolulu 96826
947-7678

Fastop
727 Waiakamilo Rd
Honolulu 96817
832-7300

Fleming Foods
91-315 Hanua St
Kapolei 96707
682-7300

Food Pantry Ltd
3536 Harding Ave
Honolulu 96816
732-5515

Foodland
55-510 Kamehameha Hwy
Laie 96762
293-4443

Foodland
Aina Haina Shopping Ctr
Honolulu 96821
373-2222

Foodland
Koko Marina Shopping
Center
Honolulu 96825
395-3131

Foodland
823 California
Wahiawa 96786
621-7411

Foodland
59-720 Kamehameha
Hwy.
Haleiwa 96712
621-7411

Foodland
95-221 Kipapa Dr.
Mililani 96789
623-3974

Foodland
94-1040 Waipio Uka
Waipahu 96797
671-5322

Foodland
2939 Harding
Honolulu 96816
734-6303

Foodland
2295 N King St
Honolulu 96819
845-1249

Foodland
1505 Dillingham
Honolulu 96817
845-2134

Foodland Market
1460 S Beretania St
Honolulu 96814
946-4654

Foodland Market
1450 Ala Moana Blvd
Honolulu 96814
949-5044

Foodland Super Market
Windward City Shopping
Center
Kaneohe 96744
247-3357

Foodland Super Market
850 Kamehameha Hwy
Pearl City 96782
455-3213

Foodland Super Market
414 N School St
Honolulu 96817
533-1398

Foodland Super Market
Ewa Beach Shopping
Center
Ewa Beach 96706
689-8383

Fred's Produce Co
1605 Colburn St
Honolulu 96817
847-3575

Frozen Foods Hawaii
2915 Kaihikapu St
Honolulu, HI 96819
839-5121

H & W Foods
1535 Colburn
Honolulu 96817
832-0350

Haleiwa Super Market
66-197 Kamehameha Hwy
Haleiwa 96712
637-5004

Hawaii Food Products
94-403 Ukee St
Waipahu 96797
676-9100

Hawaiian Flour Mills
703 N Nimitz Hwy
Honolulu 96817
545-2111

Hawaiian Grocery Stores
2915 Kaihikapu
Honolulu 96819
839-5121

Hawaiian Isles Kona
Coffee Co
2839 Mokumoa St
Honolulu 96819
833-2244

HFM Food Service
703 N Nimitz
Honolulu 96817
545-2111

Hickam Commisary
20 Hickam CT
Hickam AFB 96853
449-1363

Liliha Bakery
515 N Kuakini St #203
Honolulu 96817
531-1651

Lion Coffee
894 Queen St
Honolulu 96813
591-1199

Mac Farms of Hawaii
3615 Harding #207
Honolulu 96816
737-0645

Mapelli Food Distribu-
tion Co
2613 Waiwai Lp
Honolulu 96819
836-1985

Marukai Whoesale Mart
2310 Kamehameha Hwy
Honolulu 96819
845-5051

Meadow Gold Dairies
925 Cedar St
Honolulu, HI 96814
949-6161

Menehune Water
Company
99-1205 Halawa Valley
St
Aiea 96701
487-7777

Monfort Food Distribu-
tors
2613 Waiwai Lp
Honolulu 96819
836-1985

Napoleon's Bakery
94-1068 Ka Uka Blvd
Mililani 96789
677-7710

Nishimoto Trading Co
331 Libby
Honolulu 96819
832-7555

Palama Meat Co
2656 Waiwai Loop
Honolulu 96819
836-1441

Paradise Beverages
94-1450 Moaniani
Waipahu 96797
678-4000

Safeway
46-065 Kamehameha
Hwy
Kaneohe 96744
235-3337

Safeway
25 Kaneohe Bay Dr
Kailua 96734
254-2597

Safeway
1060 Keolu Dr
Kailua 96734
261-1909

Safeway
200 Hamakua Dr.
Kailua 96734
263-8871

Safeway
377 Keahole St
Honolulu 96825
396-6337

Safeway
98-1277 Kaahumanu St
Aiea 96701
487-1088

Safeway
1360 Pali Hwy
Honolulu 96813
538-3953

Safeway
1121 S Beretania St
Honolulu 96814
591-8315

Safeway
94-780 Meheula Pky B
Honolulu 96815
623-8111

Safeway
91-590 Farrington Hwy.
Kapolei 96707
674-0070

Safeway
94-050 Farrington Hwy
Waipahu 96797
677-1555

Safeway
848 Ala Lilikoi St
Honolulu 96818
839-9681

Safeway
2855 E Manoa Rd
Honolulu 96822
988-2058

Safeway Stores
680 Iwilei Rd #590
Honolulu, HI 96817
524-4554

Star Market
46-023 Kamehemeha Hwy.
Kaneohe 96744
233-1566

Star Market
95-1249 Meheula Pkwy
Mililani 96789
625-7171

Star Market
4211 Waialae Ave
Honolulu 96816
733-1366

Star Market
1620 N School St
Honolulu 96817
832-8400

Star Market
2470 S. King
Honolulu 96826
973-1666

Tamashiro Market
802 N King
Honolulu 96817
841-8047

Tamura Superette
86-032 Farrington Hwy
Waianae 96792
696-3321

Tamura's Wahiawa
440 Kilani Ave
Wahiawa 96786
622-4117

Times Super Market
45-934 Kamehameha Hwy
Kaneohe 96744
233-4622

Times Super Market
47-388 Hui Iwa
Kaneohe 96744
239-8827

Times Super Market
590 Kailua Rd
Kailua 96734
262-2366

Times Super Market
5740 Kalanianaole Hwy
Honolulu 96821
373-9883

Times Super Market
98-1264 Kaahumanu St
Pearl City 96782
487-3687

Times Super Market
99-115 Aiea Hts
Aiea 96701
488-5566

Times Super Market
1290 Beretania St
Honolulu 96814
524-5711

Times Super Market
1425 Liliha St
Honolulu 96817
536-4436

Times Super Market
94-766 Farrington Hwy
Waipahu 96797
671-0502

Times Super Market
94-615 Kupuohi
Waipahu 96797
678-6565

Times Super Market
1173 21st Ave
Honolulu 96816
732-6677

Times Super Market
3221 Waialae Ave
Honolulu 96816
733-5050

Times Super Market
2153 N King St
Honolulu 96819
847-0811

Times Super Market
1772 S King St
Honolulu 96826
955-3388

Tropic Fish & Vegetable
Center
1020 Auahi St
Honolulu 96814
591-2936

Vim 'n Vigor Foods
1450 Ala Moana Blvd
#1014
Honolulu 96814
955-3600

Waianae Store
85-863 Farrington Hwy
Waianae 96792
696-3131

Y Hata & Co
285 San Island Access
Rd
Honolulu 96819
845-3347

Yamaki Produce
670A Halekauwila St
Honolulu 96813
533-1854

Government

Federal jobs

Federal Employment
Information Center
U.S. Office of Personnel
Management
300 Ala Moana #5316
Honolulu 96813
541-2791 or 541-2784
(Neighbor Isles)

State jobs

**State Dept of Human
Resources Development**
235 S Beretania. #1100
Honolulu 96813
587-0977 or 1-800-468-
4644, ext. 70977
(Neighbor Isles)
587-1148 (TDD users)

Judiciary
417 S King
Honolulu 96813
539-4949

University of Hawai'i
Hiring is by each department

Department of Education
1390 Miller St.
Honolulu 96813
586-3420 (teachers)
586-3422 (non-teachers)

County jobs

Honolulu City and County
Department of Personnel
550 S King
Honolulu 96813
523-4301

Hawaii County
Department of Civil Service
101 Aupuni Street #133
Hilo 96720
961-8361

Maui County
Department of Personnel
Services
200 S High Street
Wailuku 96793
243-7850

Kauai County
Department of Personnel
Services
4444 Rice Street
Lihue 96766
241-6595

Hotels and resorts

Aina Kamalii Corporation
100 Holomoana St
Honolulu 96815
944-4480

Ala Moana Hotel
410 Atkinson Dr
Honolulu 96814
955-4811

Aloha Surf Hotel
444 Kanekapolei St
Honolulu 96815
923-0222

Aston Coral Reef Hotel
2299 Kuhio Ave
Honolulu 96815
922-1262

Aston Hotels & Resorts
2155 Kalakaua Ave #500
Honolulu 96815
931-1400

Aston Waikiki Beach
Tower
2470 Kalakaua
Honolulu 96815
926-6400

Aston Waikiki Beachside
Hotel
2452 Kalakaua Ave
Honolulu 96815
931-2100

Aston Waikiki Circle
2464 Kalakaua Ave
Honolulu 96815
923-1571

Best Western Plaza Hotel
3253 N Nimitz Hwy
Honolulu 96819
836-3636

Castle Resorts & Hotels
1150 S King St
Honolulu 96814
591-2235

Colony Surf Hotel
2885 Kalakaua Ave
Honolulu 96815
924-3111

Executive Centre Hotel
1088 Bishop St
Honolulu 96813
539-3000

Hale Koa Hotel
2055 Kalia Rd
Honolulu 96815
955-0555

Halekulani Hotel
2199 Kalia Rd
Honolulu 96815
923-2311

Hawaii Prince Hotel
100 Holomoana
Honolulu 96815
956-1111

Hawaiian Monarch Hotel
444 Niu St
Honolulu 96815
949-3911

Hawaiian Regent Hotel
2552 Kalakaua Ave
Honolulu 96815
922-6611

Hawaiian Waikiki Beach
Hotel
2570 Kalakaua Ave
Honolulu 96815
922-2511

Hawaiiana Hotel
444 Niu St
Honolulu 96815
923-3811

Hilton Hawaiian Village
Hotel
2005 Kalia Rd
Honolulu 96815
949-4321

Holiday Inn Honolulu
International Airport
3401 N Nimitz Hwy
Honolulu 96819
836-0661

Holiday Inn Waikiki
1830 Ala Moana Blvd
Honolulu 96815
955-1111

Hyatt Regency Waikiki
2424 Kalakaua Ave
Honolulu 96815
923-1234

Ihilani Resort & Spa
92-1001 Olani St
Kapolei 96707
679-0079

Ilikai Hotel
1777 Ala Moana Blvd
Honolulu 96815
949-3811

Island Colony Hotel
445 Seaside Ave
Honolulu 96815
921-7102

Jowa Hawaii Co
1777 Ala Moana #226
Honolulu 96815
942-8607

Kahala Mandarin
Oriental Hawaii
5000 Kahala Ave
Honolulu 96816
739-8888

Kyo-Ya Co
2255 Kalakaua Ave
#200
Honolulu 96815
931-8600

Marc Resorts Hawaii
2155 Kalakaua Ave 7th
floor
Honolulu 96815
926-5900

Marc Suites Waikiki
412 Lewers St
Honolulu 96815
923-8882

Marine Surf Waikiki
Hotel
364 Seaside Ave
Honolulu 96815
923-0277

Miramar at Waikiki
2345 Kuhio Ave
Honolulu 96815
922-2077

Mitsui Fudosan
(Hawaii)
700 Bishop St #1115
Honolulu 96813
526-1186

New Otani Kaimana
Beach Hotel
2863 Kalakaua Ave
Honolulu 96815
923-1555

Ocean Resort Hotel of
Waikiki
175 Paoakalani Ave
Honolulu 96815
922-3861

Otaka
2552 Kalakaua Ave
Honolulu 96815
924-4067

Outrigger Hotels &
Resorts
2375 Kuhio Ave
Honolulu 96815
921-6600

Outrigger Islander
270 Lewers St
Honolulu 96815
923-0777

Pacific Beach Hotel
2490 Kalakaua Ave
Honolulu 96815
922-1233

Pacific Marina Inn
2628 Waiwai Lp
Honolulu 96819
836-1131

Pagoda Hotel
1525 Rycroft St
Honolulu 96814
941-6611

Pan Pacific Hoteliers
92-1001 Olani St
Kapolei 96707
679-0079

Park Shore Hotel
2586 Kalakaua Ave
Honolulu 96815
923-0411

Queen Kapiolani Hotel
150 Kapahulu Ave
Honolulu 96815
922-1941

Royal Garden at Waikiki
440 Olohana
Honolulu 96815
943-0202

Royal Hawaiian Hotel
2259 Kalakaua Ave
Honolulu 96815
923-7311

Sheraton Hotels In Hawaii
2155 Kalakaua Ave
Honolulu 96815
931-8292

Turtle Bay Hilton Golf &
Tennis Resort
57-091 Kamehameha Hwy
Kahuku 96731
293-8811

Waikiki Beachcomber
Hotel
2300 Kalakaua Ave
Honolulu 96815
922-4646

Waikiki Joy Hotel
320 Lewers St
Honolulu 96815
923-2300

Waikiki Parc Hotel
2233 Helumoa Rd
Honolulu 96815
921-7272

Waikiki Parkside Hotel
1850 Ala Moana
Honolulu 96815
955-1567

Waikiki Resort Hotel
2460 Koa Ave
Honolulu 96815
922-4911

Waikiki Sand Villa
2375 Ala Wai Blvd
Honolulu 96815
922-4744

Waikiki Village Hotel
240 Lewers St
Honolulu 96815
923-3881

Insurance

AIG Hawaii Insurance
Company
500 Ala Moana Blvd #6-
300
Honolulu 96813
545-1650

Allstate Insurance
Companies
1441 Kapiolani #1510
Honolulu 96814
942-0005

Aloha Care
1357 Kapiolani #1250
Honolulu 96814
973-1650

American Mutual Group
560 N Nimitz #207
Honolulu 96817
522-8650

Bishop Insurance of
Hawaii
680 Iwilei Rd 7th floor
Honolulu 96817
536-7351

Dai Tokyo Fire & Marine
Insurance
1600 Kalani St #1520
Honolulu 96817
951-1724

Dai Tokyo Royal State-
DTRIC
1600 Kapiolani #1520
Honolulu 96814
951-1700

Equitable Life Assurance
Society
1001 Bishop St #1450
Honolulu 96813
521-4911

Finance Insurance
1164 Bishop St #400
Honolulu 96813
522-2040

Firemans Fund Insurance
Co
1001 Bishop #1900
Honolulu 96813
523-6500

First American Title Co of
Hawaii
923 Nuuanu Ave
Honolulu 96817
524-4005

First Hawaii Title
1100 Alakea St #1600
Honolulu 96813
528-5656

First Insurance Co of
Hawaii
1100 Ward Ave
Honolulu 96814
527-7777

Grand Pacific Life
Insurance
1164 Bishop St #500
Honolulu 96813
548-3333

H M A A-Hawaii Manage-
ment Alliance
1585 Kapiolani #900
Honolulu 96814
591-0088

Hartford Insurance Group
1001 Bishop Pauahi
#1700
Honolulu 96813
546-5700

Hawaii Dental Service
700 Bishop St #700
Honolulu 96813
521-1431

Hawaii Insurance
Bureau
700 Bishop #1701
Honolulu 96813
531-2771

Hawaii Insurance
Consultants
500 Ala Moana #6-300
Honolulu 96813
543-0400

Hawaiian Insurance and
Guaranty
1001 Bishop St Pacific
5th floor
Honolulu 96813
536-2777

HMSA
818 Keeaumoku
Honolulu, HI 96814
948-5110

Island Insurance Co
1022 Bethel St
Honolulu 96813
531-1311

Island Title Corp
1132 Bishop St #400
Honolulu 96813
531-0261

John Hancock Mutual
Life Insurance
1601 Kapiolani #1200
Honolulu 96814
979-3300

Liberty Mutual Group
1601 Kapiolani # 1020
Honolulu 96814
979-2020

Lo's Trading Corp USA
1188 Bishop #3104
Honolulu 96813
528-5555

Marsh & McLennan
1099 Alakea #2200
Honolulu 96813
531-4211

Mony/Mutual of New
York
1001 Bishop Pacific
#2800
Honolulu 96813
536-6977

Mullen John & Co
677 Ala Moana Blvd
#910
Honolulu 96813
531-9733

New York Life Insur-
ance Co
841 Bishop #1400
Honolulu 96813
538-3811

Pacific Guardian Life
Insurance
1440 Kapiolani #1700
Honolulu 96814
955-2236

Primerica Financial
Services
2828 Paa St #3045
Honolulu 96819
836-4772

Prudential
1100 Alakea #2800
Honolulu 96813
599-8999

Queen's Health Care Plan
500 Ala Moana Blvd #2-
200
Honolulu 96813
522-7500

Royal Insurance Agency
819 S Beretania St
Honolulu 96813
539-1700

Security Title Corp
1164 Bishop #1100
Honolulu 96813
521-9511

State Farm Insurance
400 Kahelu Ave
Mililani 96789
627-4500

Sun Life of Canada
1311 Kapiolani #512
Honolulu 96814
591-1480

TIG Insurance Company
733 Bishop St
Honolulu 96813
537-5221

University Health Care
Associates
700 Bishop St #300
Honolulu 96813
522-5570

Legal services

Alston Hunt Floyd & Ing
1001 Bishop Pacific 18th
floor
Honolulu 96813
524-1800

Ashford & Wriston
1099 Alakea 14th floor
Honolulu 96813
539-0400

Ayabe Chong Nishimoto
Sia Nakamura
1001 Bishop Pauahi
#2500
Honolulu 96813
537-6119

Bays Deaver Hiatt
1099 Alakea 16th floor
Honolulu 96813
523-9000

Burke Sakai McPheeters
737 Bishop St #3100
Honolulu 96813
523-9833

Cades Schutte Fleming &
Wright
1000 Bishop
Honolulu 96813
521-9200

Carlsmith Ball Wichman
Case & Ichiki
1001 Bishop Pacific
#2200
Honolulu 96813
523-2500

Case Bigelow & Lombardi
737 Bishop St #2600
Mauka
Honolulu 96813
547-5400

Cronin Fried Sekiya et al
841 Bishop St #1900
Honolulu 96813
524-1433

Damon Key Bocken Leong
et al
1001 Bishop Pauahi
#1600
Honolulu 96813
531-8031

Dwyer Imanaka Schraff
Kudo
900 Fort St Mall #1800
Honolulu 96813
524-8000

Fujiyama Duffy &
Fujiyama
1001 Bishop St Pauahi
#2700
Honolulu 96813
536-0802

Goodsill Anderson Quinn
Stifel
1099 Alakea 18th floor
Honolulu 96813
547-5600

Industrial Indemnity
Company
201 Merchant St #1800
Honolulu 96813
521-1477

Kobayashi Sugita & Goda
999 Bishop St #2600
Honolulu 96813
539-8700

Legal Aid Society of
Hawaii
1108 Nuuanu Ave
Honolulu 96817
536-4302

McCorriston Miho
Miller
500 Ala Moana 5
Waterfront 4th floor
Honolulu 96813
529-7300

Nakamura Elisha &
Lahne
707 Richards St 8th
floor
Honolulu 96813
523-7021

Reinwald O'Connor &
Playdon
733 Bishop #2400
Honolulu 96813
524-8350

Rush Moore Craven
Sutton et al
745 Fort St #2000
Honolulu 96813
521-0400

Torkildson Katz Fonseca
Jaffe et al
700 Bishop #1500
Honolulu 96813
523-6000

Watanabe Ing &
Kawashima
999 Bishop St #2300
Honolulu 96813
544-8300

Manufacturing: clothes

Crazy Shirts
99-969 Iwaena St
Aiea 96701
487-9919

Hilo Hattie's - Pomare
700 N Nimitz Hwy
Honolulu 96817
524-3966

Iolani Sportswear
1234 Kona St
Honolulu 96814
597-1044

Island Snow Hawaii
229 Paoakalani Ave
Honolulu 96815
926-1815

Jams World
1451 Kalani St
Honolulu 96817
847-5985

Malihini Sportswear
431 Kuwili St 3rd floor
Honolulu 96817
536-3725

Princess Kaiulani Fashions
1222 Kaumualii
Honolulu 96817
847-4806

Reyn Spooner
500 Alakawa #102B
Honolulu 96817
841-3615

Richard Tori
1334 Moonui St
Honolulu 96817
847-7041

Town & Country Surf
Shop
99-1295 Waiua Pl #2-A
Aiea 96701
483-8383

You & Me Naturally
94-076 Leokane
Waipahu 96797
671-7486

Manufacturing: food

Coca-Cola Bottling Co
949 Mapunapuna St
Honolulu 96819
839-6711

Diamond Bakery Co
756 Moowa
Honolulu 96817
847-3551

Ewa Brand Chicken
1818 Kanakanui St
Honolulu 96819
841-2828

Foremost Dairies
Hawaii
2277 Kamehameha Hwy
Honolulu 96819
841-5831

Frito-Lay
99-1260 Iwaena St
Aiea 96701
487-1515

H P C Foods
288 Libby
Honolulu 96819
848-2431

Hawaiian Host Chocolates
500 Alakawa St #111
Honolulu 96817
848-0500

Hawaiian King Candies
550 Paiea #501
Honolulu 96819
833-0041

Hawaiian Sun Products
259 Sand Is Access Rd
Honolulu 96819
845-3211

Holsum Oroweat Bakers
98-736 Moanalua Lp
Aiea 96701
488-6871

House Foods
2277 Kamehameha Hwy
Honolulu 96819
841-5831

Ito-En USA
125 Puuhale Rd
Honolulu 96819
847-4477

Loves Bakery
911 Middle
Honolulu 96819
841-2088

Pacific Poultry Co
1818 Kanakanui
Honolulu 96819
841-2828

Patisserie
2115 S Beretania St
Honolulu 96826
941-3055

Pepsi Cola Hawaii
Box 1177
Aiea 96701
484-1777

Tokyo Bento Michiyo
2850 Paa St #2
Honolulu 96819
836-4742

Manufacturing: other

Ameron Hawaii
2344 Pahounui Dr
Honolulu 96819
832-9200

Bomat
91-400 Komohana St
Kapolei 96707
673-2000

Brewer-Environmental
Industries
311 Pacific St
Honolulu 96817
532-7400

Chevron USA/Refinery
91-480 Malakole St
Kapolei 96707
682-5711

Coco Joe's Products
401 N Cane St 2B
Wahiawa 96786
622-0481

Gaspro
2305 Kamehameha Hwy
Honolulu 96819
842-2201

Hawaiian Cement
99-1100 Halawa Valley
Aiea 96701
483-3300

Hawaiian Cement
1100 Alakea St #2300
Honolulu 96813
532-3400

Honomach
91-060 Hanua
Kapolei 96707
682-5701

HSI Mechanical
227 Puuhale
Honolulu 96819
848-6422

Island Ready-Mix
Concrete
91-047 Honua
Kapolei 96707
682-1305

Lanakila Crafts
1809 Bachelot St
Honolulu 96817
531-0555

Marisco
91-607 Malakole Rd
Kapolei 96707
682-1333

Reynolds Metals Company
91-320 Komohana St
Kapolei 96707
682-1202

Serta Mattress Co
94-134 Leowaena St
Waipahu 96797
671-4071

Simmons Co
91-489 Komohana
Kapolei 96707
682-7233

Weyerhaeuser Company
900 N Nimitz Hwy
Honolulu 96817
536-3814

Medical, health care

Aloha Nursing & Rehab
Centre
45-545 Kamehameha Hwy
Kaneohe 96744
247-2220

Ann Pearl Nursing Facility
45-181 Waikalua Rd
Kaneohe 96744
247-8558

Attention-Plus Private
Nursing
1144 10th Ave
Honolulu 96826
739-2811

Beverly Manor
1930 Kamehameha IV Rd
Honolulu 96819
847-4834

Blood Bank of Hawaii
2043 Dillingham Blvd
Honolulu 96819
845-9966

Care Resource Hawaii
702 S Beretania St #3A
Honolulu 96813
599-4999

Castle Medical Center
640 Ulukahiki St
Kailua 96734
263-5500

Central Medical Clinic
321 N Kuakini St #201
Honolulu 96817
523-8611

Diagnostic Lab Services
770 Kapiolani #100
Honolulu 96813
589-5100

Forensic & Behavioral
Sciences
1088 Bishop St #506
Honolulu 96813
537-2149

Hale Ho Aloha Nursing
Home
2670 Pacific Heights Rd
Honolulu 96813
524-1955

Hale Nani Rehabilitation
& Nursing Center
1677 Pensacola St
Honolulu 96822
537-3371

Hawaii Family Dental
Centers
500 Ala Moana #7-300
Honolulu 96813
536-1696

Hawaii Healthcare
345 Queen St #910
Honolulu 96813
531-8177

Hawaiian Eye Center
606 Kilani Ave
Wahiawa 96786
621-8448

Honolulu Medical Group
550 S Beretania St
Honolulu 96813
537-2211

Interim Healthcare
1441 Kapiolani #1320
Honolulu 96814
955-1102

Island Nursing Home
1205 Alexander St
Honolulu 96826
946-5027

Kahi Mohala Hospital
91-2301 Fort Weaver Rd
Ewa Beach 96706
671-8511

Kahuku Hospital
56-117 Pualalei St
Kahuku 96731
293-9221

Kaiser Koolau Clinic
45-602 Kamehameha
Hwy
Kaneohe 96744
235-7100

Kaiser Permanente
Medical Care
3288 Moanalua Rd
Honolulu 96819
834-9094

Kaiser Permanente
Medical Group
1010 Pensacola St
Honolulu 96814
545-2950

Kaiser Punawai Clinic
94-235 Leoku St
Waipahu 96797
677-5888

Kalihi-Palama Health
Center
915 N King St
Honolulu 96817
848-1438

Kapiolani Health
55 Merchant St #2700
Honolulu 96813
535-7401

Kapiolani Medical
Center at Pali Momi
98-1079 Moanalua Rd
Aiea 96701
486-6000

Kapiolani Medical
Center for Women and
Children
1319 Punahou
Honolulu 96826
983-6000

Kuakini Medical Center
347 N Kuakini St
Honolulu 96817
536-2236

Leahi Hospital
3675 Kilauea Ave
Honolulu 96816
733-8000

Leeward Nursing Home
84-390 Jade St
Waianae 96792
695-9508

Liliha Healthcare Center
1814 Liliha St
Honolulu 96817
537-9557

Maunalani Nursing
Center
5113 Maunalani Cir
Honolulu 96816
732-0771

Nuuanu Hale Hospital
2900 Pali Hwy
Honolulu 96817
595-6311

Oahu Care Facility
1808 S Beretania St
Honolulu 96826
973-1900

Orthopedic Associates of
Hawaii
1380 Lusitana #608
Honolulu 96813
536-2261

Pearl City Medical
Association
98-1079 Moanalua Rd
#500
Aiea 96701
488-1943

Pearl City Nursing Home
919 Lehua Ave
Pearl City 96782
453-1919

Pohai Nani Good Samari-
tan Kauhale
45-090 Namoku St
Kaneohe 96744
247-6211

Prime Care Services
Hawaii
1650 Liliha St
Honolulu 96817
531-0050

Queen's Health System
1099 Alakea St #1100
Honolulu 96813
532-6100

Queen's Medical Center
1301 Punchbowl St
Honolulu 96813
538-9011

Rehabilitation Hospital of
the Pacific
226 N Kuakini St
Honolulu 96817
531-3511

Shriners Hospital for
Crippled Children
1310 Punahou
Honolulu 96826
941-4466

St Francis Medical Center
2230 Liliha
Honolulu 96817
547-6011

St Francis Medical Center
West
91-2141 Fort Weaver Rd
Ewa Beach 96706
678-7000

Straub Clinic & Hospital
888 S King St
Honolulu 96813
522-4000

Tripler Army Medical
Center
1 Jarrett White Rd
Honolulu 96859
433-6661

Wahiawa General Hospital
128 Lehua
Wahiawa 96786
621-8411

Waianae Coast Compre-
hensive Health Center
86-260 Farrington Hwy
Waianae 96792
696-7081

News media, broadcasting, publishing

Hawaii Hochi
917 Kokea
Honolulu 96817
845-2255

Hawaii Newspaper
Agency
605 Kapiolani Blvd
Honolulu 96813
525-8000

Honolulu Advertiser
605 Kapiolani Blvd
Honolulu 96813
525-8090

Honolulu Star-Bulletin
605 Kapiolani Blvd
Honolulu 96813
525-8640

RFD Publications
45-525 Luluku Rd
Kaneohe 96744
235-5881

KCCN
900 Fort St #400
Honolulu 96813
536-2728

KGMB-TV
1534 Kapiolani Blvd
Honolulu 96814
973-5462

KHNL-TV
150 Puuhale Rd
Honolulu, HI 96819
847-3246

KHON-TV
1170 Auahi St
Honolulu 96814
591-2222

KIKI
345 Queen St #601
Honolulu 96813
531-4602

KITV
801 S King St
Honolulu, HI 96813
535-0400

KSSK
1505 Dillingham Blvd
#208
Honolulu 96817
841-8300

Oceanic Cable
200 Akamainui
Mililani 96789
625-2100

Non-profits, social services, labor unions, business and professional organizations

Alu Like
567 S King St
Honolulu 96813
536-4494

American Red Cross
4155 Diamond Head Rd
Honolulu 96816
734-2101

Arcadia Retirement
Residence
1434 Punahou St
Honolulu 96822
941-0941

Bishop Museum &
Planetarium
1525 Bernice
Honolulu 96817
847-3511

Boys & Girls Club of
Honolulu
1704 Waiola St
Honolulu 96826
949-4743

Carpenters Union Local
745
1311 Houghtailing
Honolulu 96817
847-5761

Catholic Charities
250 N Vineyard St
Honolulu 96817
537-6321

Central Union Church
1660 S Beretania St
Honolulu 96826
941-0957

Child & Family Service
200 N Vineyard Blvd
Honolulu 96817
521-2377

Goodwill Industries of
Honolulu
2610 Kilihau St
Honolulu 96819
836-0313

HGEA
888 Mililani
Honolulu 96813
536-2351

Honolulu Academy of Arts
900 S Beretania St
Honolulu 96814
532-8700

Honolulu Community
Action Program
1120 Maunakea #280
Honolulu 96817
521-4531

Honolulu Symphony
Society
680 Iwilei Rd #202
Honolulu 96817
524-0815

Moiliili Community Center
2535 S King St
Honolulu 96826
955-1555

Pacific Club
1451 Queen Emma St
Honolulu 96813
536-0836

Palolo Chinese Home
Eldercare
2459 10th Ave
Honolulu 96816
737-7231

Parent Child Center
1445 Linapuni St #117A
Honolulu 96819
842-5996

Parents & Children
Together
1475 Linapuni #117-A
Honolulu 96819
847-3285

Salvation Army Family
845 22nd Ave
Honolulu 96816
732-2802

The ARC In Hawaii
3989 Diamond Head Rd
Honolulu 96816
737-7995

United Public Workers
1426 N School St
Honolulu 96817
847-2631

Waimano Auxillary
2201 Waimano Home Rd
Pearl City 96782
455-7847

Personal services
Laundry, beauty, mortuary

A & P Laundry
179C Sand Island Access
Honolulu 96819
842-0005

Al Phillips Cleaners
515 Lagoon Dr
Honolulu 96819
833-5806

American Linen
2727 Waiwai Lp
Honolulu 96819
834-7500

Borthwick Mortuary
1130 Maunakea
Honolulu 96817
522-5200

Borthwick/Hawaiian
Memorial
45-425 Kamehameha Hwy
Kaneohe 96744
233-4400

Caesars Cleaners
45-564 Kamehameha Hwy
#E
Kaneohe 96744
235-2533

Clean Living Dust Tex
210 Puuhale Rd #207C
Honolulu 96819
842-4811

Hakuyosha Hawaii
730 Sheridan St
Honolulu 96814
955-6116

Mililani Memorial Park
94-560 Kamehameha Hwy
Waipahu 96797
677-5631

Paul Brown Salon & Spa
1200 Ala Moana Blvd
Honolulu 96814
591-1881

Servicemaster of Hawaii
2600 Pualani Way #401
Honolulu 96815
922-1393

Stylists, The
2552 Kalakaua Ave
Honolulu 96815
923-4477

Volume Services
735 Iwilei Rd FL 2
Honolulu 96817
531-3127

United Laundry Services
2291 Alahao Pl
Honolulu 96819
842-5994

Valley of Temples
Memorial
47-200 Kahekili Hwy
Kaneohe 96744
239-8811

Young Laundry & Dry
Cleaning
1930 Auiki St
Honolulu 96819
836-1661

Printing, photocopying

Edward Enterprises
641 Waiakamilo Rd
Honolulu 96817
841-4231

Harbor Graphics
2222 Kamehameha Hwy
Honolulu 96819
842-7144

Island Printing Center
539 Cooke St
Honolulu 96813
591-2289

Fisher Printing
919 Kekaulike
Honolulu 96817
537-3966

Hawaii Newspaper Agency
605 Kapiolani Blvd
Honolulu 96813
525-8000

Kinkos Copies
1500 Kapiolani Blvd
Honolulu 96814
944-8500

Hagadone Printing Co
274 Puuhale Rd
Honolulu 96819
847-5310

HonBlue
501 Sumner St #3B1
Honolulu 96817
531-4611

Professional Image
125 Merchant St
Honolulu 96813
524-8585

Service Printers
1829 Dillingham
Honolulu 96819
841-7644

How to Get the Job You Want in Hawaii
8## Real estate, property managers, shopping centers, etc.

Aloha Tower Marketplace
1 Aloha Tower Dr #330
Honolulu 96813
536-3334

Ala Moana Center
1585 Kapiolani Blvd #800
Honolulu 96814
946-2811

Amfac/JMB Hawaii
700 Bishop St #2002
Honolulu, HI 96813
543-8900

Amfac Property Development
1001 Bishop #2475
Honolulu 96813
532-0333

Azabu USA Corp
410 Atkinson Dr #200
Honolulu 96814
944-6855

Campbell James Estate of
1001 Kamokila Blvd
Kapolei 96707
674-6674

Castle & Cooke
650 Iwilei Rd
Honolulu 96817
548-4811

Castle & Cooke Properties
650 Iwilei Rd
Honolulu 96817
548-6611

Castle & Cooke Land
650 Iwilei Rd
Honolulu 96817
548-4811

Cen Pac Properties
1150 S King St #1101
Honolulu 96814
593-2902

Century 21 Kahala Hale
4400 Kalanianaole Hwy
#C-21
Honolulu 96821
735-7888

Century 21 Realty
Specialists
1585 Kapiolani St #1530
Honolulu 96814
949-6322

Chaney Brooks &
Company
606 Coral
Honolulu 96813
544-1600

Coldwell Banker Pacific
Properties
1177 Kapiolani
Honolulu 96814
593-6485

Consolidated Resorts
2301 Kuhio Ave #218
Honolulu 96815
923-8456

East Oahu Realty
6600 Kalanianaole #114
Honolulu 96825
396-2000

Gentry Homes
Box 295
Honolulu 96809
599-5558

Gentry Pacific
Box 295
Honolulu 96809
599-8200

Haseko Hawaii
820 Mililani St #820
Honolulu 96813
536-3771

Hawaiiana Management
Co
711 Kapiolani Blvd 7th
floor
Honolulu 96813
593-9100

Horita, Herbert K Realty
2024 N King
Honolulu 96819
847-4241

Imperial of Waikiki
205 Lewers St
Honolulu 96815
923-1827

Kahala Mall
4211 Waialae Ave #33
Honolulu 96816
732-7736

Kamehameha Schools
Bishop Estate
567 S King St #200
Honolulu 96813
523-6200

Kukui Plaza Management
1255 Nuuanau Ave
Honolulu 96817
524-1255

MFD 700 Bishop
745 Fort St Mall
Honolulu 96813
526-1186

M M I Realty Services
1001 Bishop Pacific 200
Honolulu 96813
545-7500

McCormack Corp
66 Queen St #3304
Honolulu 96813
539-9600

Monroe & Friedlander
220 S King #1800
Honolulu 96813
521-2611

Pearl Highlands Center
1585 Kapiolani Blvd
#800
Honolulu 96814
946-2811

Pearlridge Center
98-1005 Moanalua Rd
Aiea 96701
488-0981

Prudential Locations
3465 Waialae Ave #400
Honolulu 96816
735-4200

Royal Aloha Vacation Club
1505 Dillingham Blvd
#212
Honolulu 96817
847-8050

Royal Hawaiian Shopping
Center
2201 Kalakaua Ave #A500
Honolulu 96815
922-0588

Savio Realty
931 University Ave #105
Honolulu 96826
942-7701

Schuler Homes
828 Fort St #400
Honolulu 96813
521-5661

Second City Property
Management
91-2002 Ft Weaver Rd #B
Ewa Beach 96706
681-3791

Shinwa Golf Hawaii Co
2255 Kuhio #1600
Honolulu 96815
926-1407

Stadium Mall
4510 Salt Lake
Honolulu 96818
488-3037

Title Guaranty Escrow
Services
235 Queen
Honolulu 96813
521-0211

Town Center of Mililani
95-1249 Meheula Pkwy
Mililani 96789
625-5233

Victoria Ward Ltd
1210 Auahi St #115
Honolulu 96814
591-8411

Waikele Center
94-849 Lumiana St
Waipahu 96797
671-6977

Waikiki Shopping Plaza
2270 Kalakaua Ave
Honolulu 96815
923-1191

Ward Warehouse
1050 Ala Moana
Honolulu 96814
591-8411

Waterhouse Properties
670 Queen St #200
Honolulu 96813
592-4800

Windward Mall
46-056 Kamehameha Hwy
Kaneohe 96744
235-1143

Waterfront Management
500 Ala Moana #2-500
Honolulu 96813
526-4030

Recreation

24 Hour Fitness
1680 Kapiolani
Honolulu 96814
973-4653

Aiea Bowl
99-115 Aiea Heights Dr
Aiea 96701
488-6854

E K Fernandez Shows
91-246 Oihana St
Kapolei 96707
682-5767

Ewa Beach International
Golf Club
91-050 Fort Weaver Rd
Ewa Beach 96706
689-8351

Hawaii Kai Golf Course
8902 Kalanianaole Hwy
Honolulu 96825
395-2358

Hawaii Prince Golf Club
91-1200 Ft Weaver
Ewa Beach 96706
944-4567

Honolulu Club
932 Ward Ave
Honolulu 96814
543-3900

Honolulu Country Club
1690 Ala Puumalu St
Honolulu 96818
833-4541

Ice Palace
4510 Salt Lake
Honolulu 96818
487-9921

Kalihi Leeward & Waianae
Bowl
2295 N King
Honolulu 96819
832-7171

Ko Olina Golf Club
92-1220 Aliinui Dr
Kapolei 96707
676-5309

Koolau Golf Course
45-550 Kionaole Rd
Kaneohe 96744
236-4653

Luana Hills Country Club
770 Auloa
Kailua 96734
262-2139

Makaha Valley Country
Club
84-627 Makaha Valley Rd
Waianae 96792
695-7111

Mid Pacific Country Club
266 Kaelepulu Dr
Kailua 96734
262-8161

Mililani Golf Club
95-176 Kuahelani Ave
Mililani 96789
623-2254

Oahu Country Club
150 Country Club Rd
Honolulu 96817
595-6331

Olomana Golf Links
41-1801 Kalanianaole
Hwy
Waimanalo 96795
259-9971

Outrigger Canoe Club
2909 Kalakaua Ave
Honolulu 96815
923-1585

Pearl Country Club of
Hawaii
98-535 Kaonohi St
Aiea 96701
487-1888

Sheraton Makaha Golf
Club
84-626 Makaha Valley
Rd
Waianae 96792
695-9511

Tihati Productions
3615 Harding Ave #509
Honolulu 96816
735-0292

Waialae Country Club
4997 Kahala Ave
Honolulu 96816
734-2151

Waikele Golf Club
94-200 Paioa Pl
Waipahu 96797
676-9000

Y M C A
1441 Pali Hwy
Honolulu 96813
531-3558

Y M C A
95-1190 Hikilaulia
Mililani 96789
625-1040

Y W C A
1040 Richards
Honolulu 96813
538-7061

Restaurants, food and beverage

3660 on the Rise
3660 Waialae Ave
Honolulu 96816
737-1177

A Pacific Cafe
1200 Ala Moana Blvd
#1
Honolulu 96814
593-0035

Alan Wong's Restaurant
1857 S King St 5th floor
Honolulu 96826
949-2526

Andrews
1088 Bishop
Honolulu 96813
539-3115

Anna Millers 24 Hour
Restaurant
98-115 Kaonohi St
Aiea 96701
487-2421

Beacon Restaurant
98-108 Lipoa Pl
Aiea 96701
488-1881

Beijing Restaurant
2301 Kalakaua Ave
Honolulu 96815
971-8833

Benihana of Tokyo
2005 Kalia Rd
Honolulu 96815
955-5955

Blue Zebra Cafe
500 Ala Moana #2A
Honolulu 96813
538-0409

Burger King-Pentagram
81 S Hotel St #216
Honolulu 96813
532-9393

Buzz's Original Steak
House
413 Kawailoa Rd
Kailua 96734
261-4661

Buzz's Steak and Lobster
225 Saratoga Rd
Honolulu 96815
923-6762

Buzzs Original Steak
House
98-751 Kuahao Pl
Pearl City 96782
487-6465

Byrons Drive In
3297 N Nimitz Hwy
Honolulu 96819
836-0541

California Pizza Kitchen
554 Pearl Ridge Shopping
Center
Aiea 96701
487-7741

California Pizza Kitchen
4211 Waialae Ave
Honolulu 96816
737-9446

California Pizza Kitchen
1910 Ala Moana #5
Honolulu 96815
955-5161

Chart House
46-336 Haiku Rd
Kaneohe 96744
247-6671

Chart House
1765 Ala Moana Blvd
Honolulu 96815
941-6669

Chelsea Catering
129 Iako Pl
Honolulu 96819
837-4000

China House Restaurant
1349 Kapiolani Blvd
Honolulu 96814
949-6622

Chuck Machado's Luaus
Bopx 89696
Honolulu 96830
951-9990

Columbia Inn
645 Kapiolani
Honolulu 96813
596-0757

Columbia Inn
3221 Waialae Ave
Honolulu 96816
732-3663

Compadres Mexican Bar
& Grill
1200 Ala Moana
Honolulu 96814
591-8307

Crouching Lion Inn
51-666 Kamehameha Hwy
Kaaawa 96730
237-8511

Denny's Restaurant
Pearlridge Shopping
Center
Aiea 96701
488-6311

Denny's Restaurant
205 Lewers
Honolulu 96815
923-8188

Denny's Restaurant
2586 Kalakaua Ave
Honolulu 96815
926-7200

Dennys Coffee Shop
2345 Kuhio Ave
Honolulu 96815
922-9522

Dixie Grill
404 Ward Ave
Honolulu 96814
596-8359

Dobbs International
Services
3210 Ualena St
Honolulu 96819
836-0533

Dot's In Wahiawa
130 Mango
Wahiawa 96786
622-4115

Duke's Restaurant & Bar
2335 Kalakaua #116
Honolulu 96815
922-2268

Dynasty Restaurant
1778 Ala Moana Blvd
Honolulu 96815
947-3771

Empress Restaurant
100 N Beretania St
Honolulu 96817
521-5055

Ezogiku
2146 Kalakaua
Honolulu 96815
923-6600

Fisherman's Wharf
1009 Ala Moana
Honolulu 96814
538-3808

Flamingo Pearl City
803 Kamehameha Hwy
Pearl City 96782
456-5946

Flamingo-Enterprises
1006 Waimanu
Honolulu 96814
593-9585

Furusato Japanese
Restaurant
1314 S King #504
Honolulu 96814
593-9464

Germaine's Luau
444 Hobron Ln #501
Honolulu 96815
947-1244

Golden Dragon Restaurant
2005 Kalia Rd
Honolulu 96815
946-5336

Grace's Inn
1296 S Beretania
Honolulu 96814
593-2202

Haagen Dazs
99-1287 Waiua Pl
Aiea 96701
487-2217

Hard Rock Cafe
1837 Kapiolani Blvd
Honolulu 96826
955-7383

Harpo's Pizza & Pasta
477 Kapahulu
Honolulu 96815
732-5525

Hatsuhana Japanese
Restaurant
2005 Kalia Rd
Honolulu 96815
946-8287

Hau Tree Lanai
2863 Kalakaua Ave
Honolulu 96815
921-7066

Hee Hing Corporation
449 Kapahulu Ave
Honolulu 96815
734-8474

Hooters
1 Aloha Tower Dr
#1127
Honolulu 96813
524-4668

Host Airport Restaurant
Honolulu International
Airport
Honolulu 96819
836-2566

Host Marriott Manage-
ment Services

Honolulu International
Airport
Honolulu 96819
836-2566

House of Hong
260A Lewers
Honolulu 96815
923-0202

Hungry Lion Coffee
Shop
1613 Nuuanu Ave
Honolulu 96817
536-1188

International In Flight
Catering Co
310 Rodgers Blvd
Honolulu 96819
836-2431

Jack In The Box
680 Iwilei Rd #530
Honolulu 96817
523-5024

Jamesons By the Sea
62-540 Kamehameha
Hwy
Haleiwa 96712
637-4336

Jarons Kailua
201A Hamakua Dr
Kailua 96734
261-4600

John Dominis Restau-
rant
43 Ahui St
Honolulu 96813
523-0955

Jumbos
1052 Ahua St
Honolulu 96819
839-1011

K C Drive Inn
1029 Kapahulu Ave
Honolulu 96816
737-5581

Karaoke Pub Hamayu
2400 Koa Ave
Honolulu 96815
926-7755

Kengos Seafood Buffet
500 Ala Moana Blvd
Honolulu 96813
533-0039

Kennys Burger House
1620 N School St
Honolulu 96817
841-0931

Keo's in Waikiki
1200 Ala Moana
Honolulu 96815
596-0020

Keo's in Waikiki
2040 Kuhio Ave
Honolulu 96815
951-9355

Kincaid's Fish Chop
Steakhouse
1050 Ala Moana Blvd
Honolulu 96814
591-2005

Kobe Japanese Steak
House
1841 Ala Moana Blvd
Honolulu 96815
941-4444

Kyo-Ya Restaurant
2057 Kalakaua Ave
Honolulu 96815
931-8600

Kyotaru Hawaii Corp
2154 Kalakaua Ave
Honolulu 96815
924-3663

Kyotaru Restaurant
98-1226 Kaahumanu St
Pearl City 96782
487-0091

Kyotaru U S A
657 Kapiolani
Honolulu 96813
593-2466

L'Italiano Restaurant
1330 Ala Moana Blvd 4th
floor
Honolulu 96814
591-0105

Legend Seafood Restau-
rant
100 N Beretania #108
Honolulu, HI 96817
532-1868

Legends In Concert
Hawaii
2233 Kalakaua Ave
Honolulu 96815
971-1400

Like Like Drive Inn
Restaurant
745 Keeaumoku St
Honolulu 96814
941-2515

Little Cafe Siam
1450 Ala Moana Blvd
Honolulu 96814
943-8424

Lobster and Crab House
2201 Kalakaua #308-B
Honolulu 96815
922-6868

Marian's Island Wide
Catering
79 Mango
Wahiawa 96786
621-6758

McDonald's Restaurants
711 Kapiolani #1600
Honolulu 96813
591-2080

Monterey Bay Canners
Fresh Seafood
98-1005 Moanalua Rd
Aiea 96701
483-3555

Moose McGillycuddy's
310 Lewers St
Honolulu 96815
923-0751

Nancy's Kitchen
94-1040 Waipio Uka St
Waipahu 96797
676-3438

Naniwa-Ya Japanese
Restaurant
2301 Kalakaua Ave
Honolulu 96815
923-7288

New Tokyo-Hawaii
Restaurant Co
286 Beachwalk Ave
Honolulu 96815
923-8411

Nicholas Nickolas
Restaurant
410 Atkinson Dr
Honolulu 96814
955-4466

Nicks Fish Market
2070 Kalakaua
Honolulu 96815
955-6333

Odoriko
2400 Koa Ave
Honolulu 96815
923-7368

Okonomiyaki Chibo
Restaurant
2201 Kalakaua #A-305
Honolulu 96815
922-9722

Old Spaghetti Factory
1050 Ala Moana Blvd
Honolulu 96814
591-2513

Original Pancake House
1414 Dillingham Blvd
Honolulu 96817
847-1496

Outrigger Chief Hut
2169 Kalia Rd
Honolulu 96815
923-3111

Paradise Cove Luau
1580 Makaloa #1230
Honolulu 96814
945-3571

Paradiso Seafood & Grill
2233 Kalakaua Ave
Honolulu 96815
926-2000

Patti's Chinese Kitchen
1450 Ala Moana
#1160K
Honolulu 96814
946-5002

Pepper's Waikiki Grill
& Bar
150 Kaiulani Ave
Honolulu 96815
926-4374

Perry's Smorgy
Restaurants
2380 Kuhio
Honolulu 96815
922-1084

Pizza Hut
Moanalua Shopping
Center
Honolulu 96818
422-0521

Planet Hollywood
2155 Kalakaua Ave
#200
Honolulu 96815
924-7877

Popeyes Chicken
1515 Dillingham Blvd
Honolulu 96817
841-4285

Red Lobster
1765 Ala Moana
Honolulu 96815
955-5656

Restaurant Gion
2255 Kalakaua Ave FL 2
Honolulu 96815
922-8877

Restaurant Suntory USA
2233 Kalakaua Ave
#307
Honolulu 96815
922-5511

Roy's Restaurant
6600 Kalanianaole Hwy
Honolulu 96825
396-7697

Royal Garden Chinese
410 Atkinson Blvd
Honolulu 96814
942-7788

Royal Steak & Seafood
House
2233 Kalakaua Ave
Honolulu 96815
922-6688

Ruth's Chris Steak
House
1200 Ala Moana Blvd
Honolulu 96814
591-9132

Ryan's Grill
500 Ala Moana Blvd
#6C
Honolulu 96813
599-3860

Saimin Haven
98-020 Kamehameha
Hwy
Aiea 96701
488-8824

Sam Choy's Diamond
Head Restaurant
449 Kapahulu
Honolulu 96815
732-8645

Sam Choy's Breakfast
Lunch and Crab
580 N Nimitz
Honolulu 96817
545-7979

Sarento's Top of the I
1777 Ala Moana Blvd
#225
Honolulu 96815
955-5559

Scoozees
1200 Ala Moana
Honolulu 96814
591-1777

Sea Lion Cafe
41-202 Kalanianaole Hwy
Waimanalo 96795
259-9911

Seafood Village
2424 Kalakaua Ave
Honolulu 96815
971-1818

Shorebird Prime Rib &
Pasta
2169 Kalia Rd
Honolulu 96815
922-2887

Sizzler
98-1059 Moanalua Rd
Aiea 96701
483-3565

Sizzler
94-790 Meheula Pkwy
Mililani 96789
623-3119

Sizzler
1465 Dillingham
Honolulu 96817
832-4666

Sizzler Restaurants
98-029 Hekaha St
Aiea 96701
483-3663

Sizzler Restaurants
94-030 Farrington Hwy
Waipahu 96797
671-7433

Sizzler Restaurants
1945 Kalakaua Blvd
Honolulu 96815
973-5685

Sizzler Steakhouse
25 Kaneohe Bay Dr
Kailua 96734
254-3727

Stuart Anderson's Cattle
Co
98-1262 Kaahumanu St
Pearl City 96782
487-0054

Stuart Anderson's Cattle
Company Restaurant
1050 Ala Moana Blvd
Honolulu 96814
591-9292

Sunset Grill
500 Ala Moana #1A
Honolulu 96813
521-4409

T G I Friday
950 Ward Ave
Honolulu 96814
523-5841

Taco Bell
Moanalua Shopping Center
Honolulu 96818
422-0521

Tanaka of Tokyo Central
2250 Kalakaua Ave
Honolulu 96815
922-4702

Tanaka of Tokyo East
131 Kaiulani Ave #3
Honolulu 96815
922-4233

Tanaka of Tokyo West
1777 Ala Moana Blvd
Honolulu 96815
945-3443

Tanioka's Seafoods &
Catering
94-903 Farrington Hwy
Waipahu 96797
671-3779

Tony Roma's
98-150 Kaonohi
Aiea 96701
487-7427

Tony Roma's
4230 Waialae Ave
Honolulu 96816
735-9595

Tony Roma's
1972 Kalakaua
Honolulu 96815
942-2121

Top of Waikiki
2270 Kalakaua Ave
Honolulu 96815
923-3877

Trellise Restaurant
2500 Kuhio Ave
Honolulu 96815
921-5566

Villa Paradiso
2201 Kalakaua
Honolulu 96815
926-1717

Waikiki Broiler
202 Lewers St
Honolulu 96815
923-8836

Wailana Coffee House
1860 Ala Moana Blvd
Honolulu 96815
955-3736

Wisteria Restaurant
1206 S King St
Honolulu 96814
591-9276

Yami Yogurt Hawaii
1314 S King #713
Honolulu 96814
593-8666

Yong Sing Restaurant
1055 Alakea St
Honolulu 96813
531-1366

Yoshitsume Restaurant
2586 Kalakaua Ave
Honolulu 96815
926-5616

Yum Yum Tree
970 N Kalaheo Ave
Kailua 96734
254-5861

Yum Yum Tree
95-1249 Meheula Pkwy
Mililani 96789
625-5555

Yum Yum Tree
4211 Waialae Ave
Honolulu 96816
733-3544

Zippys Restaurant
1765 S King St
Honolulu 96826
973-0880

Retail, wholesale and distribution: clothes stores

Aloha Born Free
Fashion
501 Sumner #401
Honolulu 96817
521-6975

Andrade
Box 2480
Honolulu 96804
971-4200

Banana Republic
1450 Ala Moana Blvd
Honolulu 96814
955-2602

Bebe Sport
307 Kamani
Honolulu 96813
597-1200

Chanel Boutique
2201 Kalakaua Ave
Honolulu 96815
923-0255

Crazy Shirts
99-969 Iwaena St
Aiea 96701
487-9919

Foot Locker
1450 Ala Moana
Honolulu 96814
944-8390

Gap, The
1450 Ala Moana
Honolulu 96814
949-1933

Hilo Hattie's - Pomare
700 N Nimitz Hwy
Honolulu 96817
524-3966

Interpacific Hawaii Retail
Group
1687 Kalauokalani Wy
Honolulu 96814
971-4200

Island Snow Hawaii
229 Paoakalani Ave
Honolulu 96815
926-1815

Jeans Warehouse
945 Queen St
Honolulu 96814
593-8256

Kramer's Men's & Boys
Wear
1450 Ala Moana
Honolulu 96814
951-0567

Lanai Sportswear
1258 Kamaile
Honolulu 96814
592-7722

Louis Vuitton Hawaii
2255 Kuhio Ave #1400
Honolulu 96815
971-8444

Nordstrom
1450 Ala Moana
Honolulu 96814
973-4620

Polo - Ralph Lauren
1450 Ala Moana
Honolulu 96814
947-7656

Princess Kaiulani Fashions
1222 Kaumualii
Honolulu 96817
847-4806

Reyn's
500 Alakawa #102B
Honolulu 96817
841-3615

Saks Fifth Avenue Off 5th
94-800 Lumiaina #501
Waipahu 96797
676-1773

Town & Country Surf
Shop
99-1295 Waiua Pl #2-A
Aiea 96701
483-8383

Watumull Enterprises
1388 Kapiolani
Honolulu 96814
942-8831

Williams Sonoma
1450 Ala Moana #2220
Honolulu 96814
951-5006

Watabe Wedding Service
2270 Kalakaua Ave FL 9
Honolulu 96815
931-4111

Retail and wholesale:
general merchandise stores, department stores, etc.

Ben Franklin - B F S
7192 Kalanianaole #A-142
Honolulu 96825
395-9429

Costco
333A Keahole St
Honolulu 96825
396-5538

Costco
4380 Lawehana St
Honolulu 96818
422-6955

DFS Hawaii
3375 Koapaka #200
Honolulu 96819
837-3000

Fort Shafter Shoppette
Ft Shafter Bldg 550
Honolulu 96858
845-9626

J C Penney
98-1025 Moanalua Rd
Aiea 96701
488-0961

J C Penney Company
1450 Ala Moana Blvd
Honolulu 96814
946-8068

K Mart
4561 Salt Lake Blvd
Honolulu 96818
486-6118

K Mart
500 N Nimitz Hwy
Honolulu 96817
528-2280

K Mart
94-825 Lumiaina St
Waipahu 96797
676-8886

Liberty House
1032 Fort Street Mall
Honolulu 96813
941-2345

Liberty House
Windward Mall
Kaneohe 96744
941-2345

Liberty House
4211 Waialae Ave
Honolulu 96816
941-2345

Liberty House
Pearlridge ShoppingCenter
Aiea 96701
941-2345

Liberty House
Ala Moana Shopping Ctr
Honolulu 96814
941-2345

Longs Drug Store
46-047 Kamehameha Hwy
Kaneohe 96744
235-4511

Longs Drug Store
377 Keahole St
Honolulu 96825
395-9491

Longs Drug Store
850 Kamehameha Hwy
Pearl City 96782
455-1087

Longs Drug Store
98-1005 Moanalua Rd
Aiea 96701
487-3641

Longs Drug Store
1330 Pali Hwy
Honolulu 96813
536-7302

Longs Drug Store
925 California Ave
Wahiawa 96786
621-6888

Longs Drug Store
94-780 Meheula Pky
Wahiawa 96786
623-6466

Longs Drug Store
94-060 Farrington Hwy
Waipahu 96797
676-8114

Longs Drug Store
4211 Waialae Ave
Honolulu 96816
732-0784

Longs Drug Store
1620 N School St
Honolulu 96817
847-5351

Longs Drug Store
2750 Woodlawn Dr
Honolulu 96822
988-2161

Longs Drug Stores
45-480 Kaneohe Bay Dr.
Kaneohe 96744
235-6451

Longs Drug Stores
591 Kailua
Kailua 96734
261-8537

Longs Drug Stores
1088 Bishop
Honolulu 96813
536-4551

Longs Drug Stores
33 S. King
Honolulu 96813
537-5688

Longs Drug Stores
95-221 Kipapa Dr.
Mililani 96789
623-2854

Longs Drug Stores
94-780A Meheula
Pkwy.
Mililani 96789
623-6466

Longs Drug Stores
95-1249D Meheula
Pkwy.
Mililani 96789
625-5211

Longs Drug Stores
91-590 Farrington Hwy.
Honolulu 96816
674-0069

Longs Drug Stores
86-120 Farrington
Waianae 96792
696-6387

Longs Drug Stores
3221 Waialae
Honolulu 96816
735-5526

Longs Drug Stores
848 Ala Lilikoi
Honolulu 96818
833-2594

Longs Drug Stores
2220 S. King
Honolulu 96826
949-4781

Longs Drugs Stores
2270 Hoonee Pl
Honolulu 96819
848-0911

Neiman Marcus
1450 Ala Moana #2101
Honolulu 96814
951-8887

Ross Stores
1000 Kamehameha Hwy
Pearl City 96782
456-1005

Salvation Army
2950 Manoa Rd
Honolulu 96822
988-2136

Sam's Club
1000 Kamehameha Hwy
#100
Pearl City 96782
456-7788

Schofield Main Exchange
Schofeld Barracks Bldg 693
Wahiawa 96786
622-1773

Sears
45-056 Kamehameha Hwy.
Kaneohe 96744
247-8211

Sears
Windmard Mall
Kaneohe 96744
247-8211

Sears
98-180 Kamehameha Hwy
Aiea 96701
487-4211

Sears
1450 Ala Moana Blvd
Honolulu 96814
947-0211

Sears Roebuck & Co
98-600 Kamehameha Hwy
#200
Pearl City 96782
453-3500

Shirokiya
Pearlridge Shopping
Center
Aiea 96701
483-7711

Shirokiya
1450 Ala Moana Blvd
Honolulu 96814
973-9111

Wal Mart
94-595 Kupuohi St
Waipahu 96789
688-0066

Wal-Mart
95-550 Lanikuhana Ave
Mililani 96789
623-6744

Retail, wholesale and distribution: other

A & E Creations
2250 Kalakaua Ave # 310
Honolulu 96815
926-8886

ABC Discount Store
1811 Ala Moana Blvd
Honolulu 96815
946-5288

Aldora Distinctive Jewelry
1777 Ala Moana
Honolulu 96815
946-9595

Aloha Catering
1448 Kalani St
Honolulu 96817
841-5041

American Carpet One
302 Sand Island Access Rd
Honolulu, HI 96819
832-2000

Anderson News
3375 Koapaka St #D180
Honolulu 96819
836-5555

Barnes & Noble
4211 Waialae Ave
Honolulu 96816
737-3323

Blockbuster Video
1221 Kapiolani Blvd #740
Honolulu 96814
591-2800

Book Jobbers Hawaii
287 Kalihi
Honolulu 96819
845-2656

Borders Books & Music
1200 Ala Moana Blvd
Honolulu 96814
591-8995

Borders Books & Music
94-821 Lumiaina
Waipahu 96797
676-6699

Cosmetic Consultants Of
2500 Kuhio Ave
Honolulu 96815
923-6353

CS Wo & Sons
702 S Beretania St
Honolulu 96813
545-5966

DFS Waikiki
330 Royal Hawaiian Ave
Honolulu 96815
931-2700

Disney Store
1450 Ala Moana #2058
Honolulu 96814
957-0050

Elephant Walk
1450 Ala Moana
Honolulu 96814
949-4011

Flora-Dec Sales
373 N Nimitz Hwy
Honolulu 96817
537-6194

G B C Boxes & Packaging
4478 Malaai St
Honolulu 96819
423-4111

Greeters of Hawaii
3375 Koapaka
Honolulu 96819
836-0161

Hawaii Business Eqpt
590A Paiea St
Honolulu 96819
834-3636

Hawaii Hotel &
Restaurant Supply
2655 Waiwai Lp
Honoluu 96819
834-2002

Hawaiian Island Creations
1450 Ala Moana #1042
Honolulu 96814
973-6780

Hawaiian Isles Distributors
2839 Mokumoa
Honolulu 96819
833-2244

Homeworld
702 S Beretania
Honolulu 96813
545-5966

Hopaco-Boise Cascade
2833 Paa St
Honolulu 96819
831-8611

IKON Office Solutions
560 N Nimitz Hwy
Honolulu 96817
521-2679

IKON Office Solutions
94-155 Leoole St 101A
Waipahu 96797
677-2678

Island Camera & Gift
Shops
670 Queen #200
Honolulu 96813
592-4848

Local Motion
424 Sumner
Honolulu 96817
523-7873

Makaala
Box 25
Honolulu 96810
839-7791

Marlin Distributors
91-312 Komohana
Kapolei 96707
682-4314

Maui Divers of Hawaii
1520 Liona
Honolulu 96814
946-7979

Mitsukoshi (USA)
2255 Kuhio Ave #920
Honolulu 96815
922-2355

Norikos Hawaii
47-525 Kamehameha
Hwy
Kaneohe 96744
239-9770

Optical Suppliers
99-1253 Halawa Vly
Aiea 96701
486-2933

Orchids of Hawaii
740 Kohou
Honolulu 96817
847-3731

Pacific Home Furnishings
98-735 Kuahao Pl
Pearl City 96782
487-3881

Pictures Plus
1000 Kamehameha #224
Pearl City 96782
453-4828

Radio Shack
1712 S King St
Honolulu 96826
946-6511

Revlon of Hawaii
2766 Waiwai Lp
Honolulu 96819
836-0191

Royal Hawaiian Heritage
1525 Kalakaua
Honolulu 96826
942-7474

Sony Hawaii Company
960 Mapunapuna
Honolulu 96819
834-6611

Sports Authority
333 Ward Ave
Honolulu 96814
596-0166

Sports Authority
94-809 Lumiaina Bldg 5
Waipahu 96797
677-9933

Sultan Company
3049 Ualena St #1400
Honolulu 96819
923-4971

Tempo Music
710 Kakoi
Honolulu 96819
837-7800

Toys R Us
98-1101 Moanalua Rd
Aiea 96701
487-5811

Trends of Hawaii
1804 Hart St
Honolulu 96819
841-8731

Twentieth Century
Furniture
Box 17068
Honolulu 96817
839-7211

Waikiki Trader Corp
2330 Kalakaua Ave
Honolulu 96815
971-2999

Waldenbooks
46-056 Kamehameha Hwy
Kaneohe 96744
235-0844

Watanabe Floral
1602 Kanakanui
Honolulu 96817
848-1026

Watanabe Floral
1607 Hart St
Honolulu 96817
848-1026

Wayne's Carpet
3025 Waialae Ave
Honolulu 96816
735-3005

Webco Hawaii
2840 Mokumoa St
Honolulu 96819
839-4551

Wyland Galleries
94-130 eokane St #2
Waipahu 96797
676-7498

Yamada K Distributors
2499 Koapaka
Honolulu 96819
836-3221

Yokohama Okadaya
2250 Kalakaua Ave #513
Honolulu, HI 96815
922-5731

Schools

Brigham Young University
Hawaii
55-220 Kulanui St
Laie 96762
293-3211

Chaminade University
3140 Waialae
Honolulu 96816
735-4711

Damien Memorial High
School
1401 Houghtailing St
Honolulu 96817
841-0195

Hanalani Schools
94-294 Anania Dr
Mililani 96789
625-0737

Hawaii Baptist Academy
High School
2429 Pali Hwy
Honolulu 96817
595-6301

Hawaii Pacific University
1166 Fort Street Mall
Honolulu 96813
544-0200

Heald College
1500 Kapiolani Blvd
Honolulu 96814
955-1500

Honolulu Community
College
874 Dillingham
Honolulu 96817
845-9211

Iolani School
563 Kamoku St
Honolulu 96826
949-5355

Kamehameha Secondary
School
210 Konia Cir
Honolulu 96817
842-8211

Kapiolani Community
College
4301 Diamond Head Rd
Honolulu 96816
734-9111

Leeward Community
College
96-045 Ala Ike
Pearl City 96782
455-0011

Maryknoll High School
1402 Punahou St
Honolulu 96822
973-1888

Mid Pacific Institute
2445 Kaala St
Honolulu 96822
973-5000

Punahou School
1601 Punahou St
Honolulu 96822
944-5711

Sacred Hearts Academy
3253 Waialae Ave
Honolulu 96816
734-5058

Special Education
Center of Hawaii
708 Palekaua St
Honolulu 96816
734-0233

St Andrews Priory
School
224 Queen Emma Sq
Honolulu 96813
536-6102

St Louis School
3142 Waialae Ave
Honolulu 96816
739-7777

University of Hawaii at
Manoa
2530 Dole St
Honolulu 96822
956-8111

University of Hawaii
West Oahu
96-043 Ala Ike
Pearl City 96782
453-6565

Windward Community
College
45-720 Keaahala Rd
Kaneohe 96744
235-0077

Telecommunications

Adtech
3465 Waialae Ave #200
Honolulu 96816
734-3300

Aeronautical Radio
2668 Waiwai Lp
Honolulu 96819
831-4800

Aloha Conferencing
1001 Bishop St Pauahi
1800
Honolulu 96813
523-1111

AT&T Corp
500 Ala Moana #1-400
Honolulu 96813
526-6640

Bell Atlantic Prof
Services
1369 Colburn Stt
Honolulu 96817
845-0403

Communication
Consulting Services
1136 Union Mall #401
Honolulu 96813
536-6677

Digital Island
1132 Bishop #1001
Honolulu 96813
540-4000

Digitel
1000 Bishop #200
Honolulu 96813
547-2500

G S T
737 Bishop St
Honolulu 96813
791-1000

G T E Hawaiian Tel
1177 Bishop St
Honolulu 96813
546-4511

G T E Wireless
733 Bishop #1900
Honolulu 96813
536-4848

GTE Mobilenet
733 Bishop St #1900
Honolulu 96813
536-4848

Hawaiian Wireless
707 Richards #508
Honolulu 96813
540-3500

Honolulu Cellular
Telephone Co
500 Kahelu Ave
Mililani 96789
625-8646

Long Distance USA/Sprint
925 Dillingham Blvd
Honolulu 96817
847-2121

Lucent Technology
3375 Koapaka St #G314
Honolulu 96819
839-29596

Pacific Service Technolo-
gies
3375 Koapaka St #D-160
Honolulu 96819
833-3778

PrimeCo Personal
Communications
1132 Bishop 11th floor
Honolulu 96813
566-9400

Progressive Communica-
tions
518 Holokahana Ln
Honolulu 96817
521-0000

Ram Paging Hawaii
1050 Queen St
Honolulu 96814
593-2337

S A I C Hawaii
3049 Ualena St #1001
Honolulu 96819
831-1800

Science & Technology
International
1733 Bishop 31st floor
Honolulu 96813
540-4700

Sprint Hawaii
925 Dillingham
Honolulu 96817
841-4144

VoiceStream Wireless
1100 Alakea #101
Honolulu 96813
522-1470

Wheat International
Communications
733 Bishop St #1820
Honolulu 96813
521-8810

Transportation, shipping, storage, etc.

Air Service Hawaii
95 Nakolo Pl
Honolulu 96819
839-5003

Aloha Airlinies
Box 30028
Honolulu 96820
836-4185

700 BISHOP ST. #800

American Hawaii Cruises
~~2100 N Nimitz Hwy~~
Honolulu 96819 *3*
~~847-3172~~ *538-7601*

9-1 pm.

American International
Cargo
110 Keehi Pl
Honolulu 96819
836-0656

American Movers
94-1489 Moaniani
Waipahu 96797
676-6683

AMR Services Corporation
300 Rodgers
Honolulu 96819
839-0202

Atlas Van Lines
94-360 Ukee St
Waipahu 96797
676-9120

Baggage Transfer Service
522 Ekolu Way
Honolulu 96819
845-7804

Bekins Hawaiian Movers
91-241 Kalaeloa Blvd
Kapolei 96707
682-6055

Chun Kim Chow
255 Sand Island Access Rd
Honolulu 96819
532-5725

City Wide Transportation
Co
933 N Nimitz Hwy #A
Honolulu 96817
599-7950

Coleman American
Companies
91-242 Kalaeloa Blvd
Kapolei 96707
682-1576

Crown Pacific Hawaii
600 Kahelu Ave
Mililani 96789
625-4520

DHX-Dependable
Hawaiian Express
5 Sand Is Access Rd
Honolulu 96819
841-7311

Dyer, M & Sons
98-054 Kuleana Rd
Pearl City 96782
456-4200

DynAir Corp
300 Rodgers #63
Honolulu 96819
834-1057

Federal Express Corp
129 Pohakulana Pl
Honolulu 96819
463-3339

Gomes School Bus
Service
47-114 Wailehua Rd
Kaneohe 96744
239-6755

Hallmark Aviation Svrs
Honolulu International
Airport
Honolulu 96819
833-6636

Hawaii Air Ambulance
Box 30242
Honolulu 96820
836-2000

Hawaii Stevedores
965 N Nimitz Hwy
Honolulu 96817
527-3400

Hawaii Transfer Co
94-1420 Moaniani
Waipahu 96797
677-3111

Hawaiian Airlines
Box 3008
Honolulu 96820
835-3950

Hawaiian Tug & Barge
Corp
Box 3288
Honolulu 96801
543-9311

Honolulu Transfer &
Storage
1122 Mikole St
Honolulu 96819
841-3633

Island Air
99 Kapalulu Pl
Honolulu 96819
836-7693

Island Movers
Box 17865
Honolulu 96817
848-5200

J C Penney Company
716 Umi St
Honolulu 96819
847-5711

Kams Express
802 Mapunapuna St
Honolulu 96819
839-2735

M Dyer & Sons
98-054 Kuleana Rd
Pearl City 96782
456-4200

Martin Warehousing &
Distribution
2340B Kamehameha
Hwy
Honolulu 96819
841-8999

Matson Navigation Co
Sand Island Access Rd
Honolulu 96817
848-1211

McCabe Hamilton &
Renny Co
1130 N Nimitz #A265
Honolulu 96817
524-3255

Oahu Transit Services
811 Middle St
Honolulu 96819
848-4400

Pacific Transfer &
Warehouse
94-360 Ukee St
Waipahu 96797
676-9120

Rocky's Limousine
Service
975 Kapiolani Blvd
Honolulu 96814
596-8488

Royal Hawaiian Cruises
Box 29816
Honolulu 96820
848-6360   848-6279 Fx
ATTN: LEILA

Sause Brothers Ocean
Towing Co
Pier 20
Honolulu 96817
521-5082

Sida of Hawaii
439 Kalewa
Honolulu 96819
836-3535

Tanaka, H Trucking
Service
1064 Sand Island Parkway
Honolulu 96819
845-2424

Terminal Transportation
443 Kalewa
Honolulu 96819
836-3186

Touchdown Trucking
4321 Lawehana St
Honolulu 96818
423-8777

United Parcel Service
Box 31247
Honolulu 96820
839-1907

Worldwide Moving &
Storage
Box 29849
Honolulu 96820
682-3722

Young Brothers
705 N Nimitz Hwy
Honolulu 96817
543-9311

Travel agency, tour operators, tourism

Airport Motorcoach
Service
443 Kalewa St
Honolulu 96819
839-0911

Aloha 7 Travel Agency
2255 Kuhio Ave #1700
Honolulu 96815
921-3333

Aloha State Tour &
Transportation Co
1060 Puuwai
Honolulu 96819
841-8031

Aloha V I P Tours
444 Hobron Ln #500
Honolulu 96815
955-5900

American Express Travel
1221 Kapiolani #400
Honolulu 96814
596-3700

Appreciate Hawaii Tours
2255 Kuhio Ave #710
Honolulu 96815
922-1100

Atlantis Submarines
1600 Kapiolani #1630
Honolulu 96814
973-9800

Cheap Tickets
1440 Kapiolani #800
Honolulu 96814
945-7439

Discovery Aloha
2155 Kalakaua Ave #620
Honolulu 96815
926-4716

E Noa Tours
1141 Waimanu St
Honolulu 96814
593-8073

Hawaii Convention Center
1801 Kalakaua
Honolulu 96815
943-3500

Hawaii Visitors &
Convention Bureau
2270 Kalakaua #801
Honolulu 96815
923-1811

J T B Hawaii
2155 Kalakaua 9th floor
Honolulu 96815
922-0200

Jetour
2255 Kuhio Ave #700
Honolulu 96815
926-1551

Kauai Island Tours/Waikiki
2222 Kalakaua #1414
Honolulu 96815
922-2391

Kintetsu International
Express (USA)
2270 Kalakaua #1400
Honolulu 96815
923-1926

Leisure Tours
2222 Kalakaua Ave #1310
Honolulu 96815
922-1636

M C & A
615 Piikoi St #1000
Honolulu, HI 96814
589-5500

M L T Northwest World
Vacations
444 Hobron Ln 5th
floor
Honolulu 96815
941-7977

M T I Vacations
1860 Ala Moana #400
Honolulu 96815
943-1143

MTI Vacations
1860 Ala Moana Blvd
#400
Honolulu 96815
943-1143

N T A Pacific -Nippon
Travel
711 Kapiolani #1000
Honolulu 96813
596-4200

Nippon Express Hawaii
2270 Kalakaua
Honolulu 96815
922-5795

NTA Pacific
711 Kapiolani Blvd
#1000
Honolulu 96813
596-4200

Ocean Express Hawaii
1600 Kapiolani #1000
Honolulu 96814
947-1212

Outrigger Islander
2222 Kalakaua #800
Honolulu 96815
926-1833

Pacifico Creative
Service
2270 Kalakaua Ave
#1600
Honolulu 96815
926-4500

Panda Travel
1017 Kapahulu Ave
2nd floor
Honolulu 96816
734-1961

Paradise Cruise
1540 S King St
Honolulu 96814
983-7700

Pleasant Hawaiian
Holidays
2222 Kalakaua Ave
16th floor
Honolulu 96815
926-1833

Polynesian Adventure
Tours
1049 Kikowaena Pl
Honolulu 96819
833-9600

Polynesian Cultural Center
55-370 Kamehameha Hwy
Laie 96762
293-3000

Polynesian Hospitality
650 Iwilei
Honolulu 96817
524-5040

R & C Hawaii Tours
1722 Kalakaua #300
Honolulu 96826
942-3333

Regal Travel
720 Iwilei #101
Honolulu 96817
566-7000

Roberts Hawaii Tours
680 Iwilei Rd #700
Honolulu 96817
523-7750

Sea Life Park
41-202 Kalanianaole
Waimanalo 96795
259-7933

Trans Hawaiian Services
720 Iwilei Rd #101
Honolulu 96817
566-7000

Trans Quality
2781 Waiwai Loop
Honolulu 96819
839-4644

Trans-Orbit Hawaii
2255 Kuhio Ave #1020
Honolulu 96815
971-0123

Travel Plaza
2270 Kalakaua Ave #1200
Honolulu 96815
921-9500

Voyager Submarines
1085 Ala Moana Blvd
#104
Honolulu 96814
592-7850

Waikiki Trolley Tours
1141 Waimanu #152
Honolulu 96814
593-8750

Waimea Valley and
Adventure Park
59-864 Kamehameha Hwy
Haleiwa 96712
638-8511

Hawaii Island top companies

Agriculture

C Brewer & Co
Box 1826
Papaikou 96781
969-1826

Cyanotech Corp
73-4460 Queen
Kaahumanu #102
Kailua-Kona 96740
326-1353

Kau Agribusiness Co Inc
Box 130
Pahala 96777
928-8311

Mac Farms of Hawaii Inc
89-406 Mamalahoa Hwy
Captain Cook 96704
328-2435

Mauna Kea Agribusiness
Co
Box 4190
Hilo 96721
964-1011

Parker Ranch
Box 458
Kamuela 96743
885-7311

Tropical Connection
Box 9
Pahoa 96778
965-8444

Tropical Hawaiian
Products
Box 210
Keaau 96749
966-7435

Automotive

Alamo
Box 4449
Kailua-Kona 96745
329-8896

Alamo
Hilo Airport
Hilo 96720
961-3343

Avis Rent a Car Systems
Keahole Airport Box 687
Kailua-Kona 96745
327-3000

Avis Rent a Car Systems
Lyman Field
Hilo 96720
935-1290

Big Island Toyota
811 Kanoelehua Ave
Hilo 96720
935-2258
935-2920

Budget Rent A Car Hawaii
Box 4938
Hilo 96720
935-6878

Budget Rent-A-Car
Systems Inc
Keahole Airport
Kailua-Kona 96745
329-8511

Dollar Rent a Car
Box 2548
Kailua-Kona 96745
329-2744

Hawaii Motors
1177 Kilauea
Hilo 96721
961-5222

Hertz
Keahole Airport
Kailua-Kona 96740
329-3566

I K Motors Inc
400 E Kawili St
Hilo 96720
935-3741

Orchid Isle Auto Center
76-6319 Kuakini Hwy
Kailua-Kona 96740
329-4851

Orchid Isle Auto Center
1030 Kanoelehua Ave
Hilo 96720
935-1191

Building cleaners

C W Maintenance Inc
56 Wiwoole
Hilo 96720
935-8543

Contractors

Isemoto Contracting Co
74-5039B Queen
Kaahumanu Hwy
Kailua-Kona 96740
329-8051

Isemoto Contracting Co
648 Piilani St
Hilo 96720
935-7194

JAS W Glover
890 Leilani St
Hilo 96720
935-0871

Kaiza Construction Inc
Box 1690
Kailua-Kona 96745
325-6951

M Sonomura Contract-
ing Co
100 Kukila St
Hilo 96720
935-8561

Maryl Group Inc
Box 1928
Kailua-Kona 96745
322-7890

Y S Rock
733 Kannoelehua Ave
Hilo 96720
933-8480

Willocks Construction
Corp
16-209 Melekahiwa Pl
Keaau 96749
982-9099

Construction, building supplies

HPM Building Supply
380 Kanoelehua Ave
Hilo 96720
935-0875

Detective, security

Freeman Guards
22 Furneaux Ln
Hilo 96720
961-2755

Hawaii Protective Assn
159 Keawe St
Hilo 96720
935-3621

Diversified

C Brewer & Co
Box 1826
Papaikou 96781
969-1826

Maryl Group Inc
Box 1928
Kailua-Kona 96745
322-7890

Parker Ranch
Box 458
Kamuela 96743
885-7311

Detective, security

HSI Corp
400 Hualani St Ste 195B
Hilo 96720
935-3934

Diversified, conglomerates

Kitagawa, I & Co
400 E Kawili St
Hilo 96720
935-3741

Electric

Hawaii Electric Light
Company
1200 Kilauea Ave
Hilo 96720
935-1171

Financial institutions

Bank of Hawaii
75-5595 Palani Rd
Kailua-Kona 96740
326-3900

Bank of Hawaii
120 Pauahi St
Hilo 96720
935-9701

Big Island Educational
FCU
66 Lono St
Hilo 96720
935-9778

First Hawaiian Bank
1205 Kilauea Ave
Hilo 96720
933-2260

Hawaii Community FCU
81-6631 Mamalalahoa
Hwy
Kealakekua 96750
322-9666

Hawaii Federal and State
Empoyees FCU
632 Kinoole St
Hilo 96720
961-2666

JCC FCU
476 Hinano St
Hilo 96720
933-6700

Food and beverage

Suisan Co
Box 366
Hilo 96721
935--8511

Hotels, resorts

Four Seasons Resort
Hualalai
100 Kaupulehu Dr
Kaupulehu 96740
874-8000
325-8400

Hapuna Beach Prince
Hotel
62-100 Kaunaoa Dr
Kamuela 96743
882-5770

Hawaii Naniloa Resort
93 Banyan Dr
Hilo 96720
969-3333

Hilo Hawaiian Hotel
71 Banyan Dr
Hilo 96720
935-9361

Hilo Seaside Hotel
126 Banyan Way
Hilo 96720
935-0821

Hilton Waikoloa Village
69-425 Waikoloa Beach Dr
Waikoloa 96738
886-1234

Keauhou Beach Hotel
78-6740 Alii Dr
Kailua-Kona 96740
322-3441

King Kamehameha's Kona
Beach Hotel
75-5660 Palani Rd
Kailua-Kona 96740
329-2911

Kona Bay Hotel
75-5739 Alii Dr
Kailua-Kona 96740
329-1393

Kona Coast Resort
78-6842 Alii Dr
Keauhou 96739
324-1721

Kona Islander Inn
75-5776 Kuakini Hwy
Kailua-Kona 96740
329-3181

Kona Seaside Hotel
75-5646 Palani Rd
Kailua-Kona 96740
329-2455

Kona Surf Resort
78-128 Ehukai St
Kailua-Kona 96740
322-3411

Kona Village Resort
PO Box 1299
Kailua-Kona 96745
325-5555

Mauna Kea Beach Hotel
62-100 Mauna Kea
Beach Dr
Kamuela 96743
882-7222

Mauna Lani Bay Hotel
& Bungalows
68-1400 Mauna Lani Dr
Kamuela 96743
885-6622

Mauna Lani Point
68-1310 Maunalani Dr
Kamuela 96743
885-5022

Mauna Lani Resort
68-1310 Maunalani Dr
Kohala Coast 96743
885-6677

Orchid at Mauna Lani
1 N Kaniku Dr
Kamuela 96743
885-2000

Royal Kona Resort
75-5852 Alii Dr
Kailua-Kona 96740
329-3111

Royal Waikoloan
69-275 Waikoloa Beach
Dr
Waikoloa 96738
886-6789

Volcano House
Box 53
Hawaii National Park
96718
967-7321

Waikoloa Beach Resort
1020 Keana Pl
Kamuela 96743
886-1000

Manufacturing: food

Big Island Candies Inc
500 Kalanianaole Ave
Hilo 96720
961-2199

Mauna Loa Macadamia
Nut Corp
HC 01 Box 3
Hilo 96720
982-6562

Medical care

Clinical Laboratories of
Hawaii
33 Lanihuli
Hilo 96720
935-4814

Hale Anuenue Restor-
ative Care Center
1333 Waianuenue Ave
Hilo 96720
961-6644

Hilo Medical Center
1190 Waianuenue Ave
Hilo 96720
974-4700

Hospice of Hilo
1266 Waianuenue Ave
Hilo 96720
969-1733

Keauhou Rehab &
Health Care Ctr
78-6957 Kamehameha
III Rd
Kailua-Kona 96740
322-2790

Kona Community Hospital
Haukapili St
Kealakekua 96750
322-9311

Life Care Center of Hilo
944 W Kawailani St
Hilo 96720
959-9151

Real estate

Clark Realty Corp
75-5722 Kuakini Hwy
#103
Kailua-Kona 96740
329-5255

Keauhou Resort Co
78-6740 Makolea
Kailua-Kona 96740
322-2708

Realty Investment Co
345 Kekuanaoa St
Hilo 96720
961-5252

Transcontinental Dev Co
150 Waikoloa Beach Dr
Kamuela 96743
885-1000

Recreation

Kapalua Golf Club
300 Kapalua Dr
Honokaa 96727
669-8870

Kona Country Club
78-7000 Alii Dr
Kailua-Kona 96740
322-3431

Red Sails Sports Hawaii
69-425 Waikoloa Beach
Rd
Kamuela 96743
8852876

Seamountain Golf Course
Box 190
Pahala 96777
928-6233

Waikoloa Beach Golf Club
1020 Keana Pl
Kamuela 96743
885-6060

YWCA
145 Ululani St
Hilo 96720
935-7141

Restaurant

Cafe Pesto Hilo Bay
308 Kamehameha Ave
Hilo 96720
969-6640

Chart House
75-5770 Alii Dr
Kailua-Kona 96740
329-2451

Denny's
75-1027 Henry
Kailua-Kona 96740
334-1313

Fiascos
200 Kanoelehua Ave
Hilo 96720
935-7666

Hard Rock Cafe
75-5801 Alii Dr
Kailua-Kona 96740
329-8866

Huggos Restaurant
75-5828 Kahakai Rd
Kailua-Kona 96740
329-1493

Jolly Roger Kona
75-5776 Alii Dr
Kailua-Kona 96740
329-1344

Kona Inn Restaurant
75-5744 Alii Dr
Kailua-Kona 96740
329-4455

Kona Ranch House
75-5653 Ololi Rd
Kailua-Kona 96740
329-7061

Marriott Food Services
523 W Lanikaula St
Hilo 96720
933-3303

Ocean View Inn
75-5683 Alii Dr
Kailua-Kona 96745
329-9998

Roy's Waikoloa
250 Waikoloa Beach Dr
Waikoloa 96738
885-4321

Sam Choy's Kaloko
73-5576 Kauhola St
Kailua-Kona 96740
326-1545

Scruffles
1438 Kilauea Ave
Hilo 96720
935-6664

Sizzler Restaurant
74-5586 Palani Rd
Kailua-Kona 96740
329-3374

Waikoloa Beach Grill
1022 Keana Pl
Waikoloa 96743
885-6131

Retail: clothes

Reyn Spooner
Box 1509
Kamuela 96743
885-7315

Retail: general merchandise

Costco
73-5600 Maiau St
Kailua-Kona 96740
331-4831

J C Penney Company Inc
111 E Puainako
Hilo 96720
959-0229

K Mart
74-5465 Kamahaeha
Kailua-Kona 96740
326-2331

Liberty House Inc
111 E Puainako St
Hilo 96720
959-3561

Longs
555 Kilauea Ave
Hilo 96720
935-3356

Longs
111 E Puainako St
Hilo 96720
959-5881

Sears
111 E Puainako St Bldg
2
Hilo 96720
981-4001

Wal Mart
75-1015 Henry St
Kailua-Kona 96740
334-0466

Wal Mart
325 E Makaala
Hilo 96720
967-9115

Retail: grocer

KTA Super Market
Box 246
Kailua-Kona 96745
329-1677

KTA Super Stores
Kona Coast Shopping
Ctr
Kailua-Kona 96740
329-1677

KTA Super Stores
50 E Puainako St
Hilo 96720
959-4575

KTA Super Stores
Box 1881
Hilo 96721
959-9111

Manono Mini Mart
454 Manono St
Hilo 96720
935-0611

Miko Meat Co
230 Kekuanaoa St
Hilo 96720
935-0841

Sack n Save Foods
2100 Kanoelehua Ave
Hilo 96720
959-5831

Safeway
111 E Puainako St
Hilo 96720
959-3502

Sure Save Supermarkets
16-204 Melekahiwa Pl
Keaau 96749
966-5411

Retail: other

Borders Books & Music
75-100 Henry St
Kailua-Kona 96740
331-1668

Borders Books & Music
301 Makaala St
Hilo 96720
933-1410

Floral Resources/Hawaii
Inc
175 E Kawailani St
Hilo 96720
959-5851

Schools

Hale Kakoo Punana Leo
1744 Kinoole St
Hilo 96720
959-4979

Hawaii Community
College
200 W Kawili
Hilo 96720
974-7311

Hawaii Preparatory
Academy
Box 428
Kamuela 96743
885-7321

St Joseph Jr Sr High
School
1000 Ululani St
Hilo 96720
935-4936

University of Hawaii Hilo
200 W Kawili
Hilo 96720
974-7311

Telecommunications

GTE Hawaiian Telephone
Co Inc
161 Kinoole
Hilo 96720
933-6514

Transportation

H T & T Co Inc
888 Kalanianaole
Hilo 96720
933-7700

Laupahoehoe Transporta-
tion Co
35 Holomua St
Hilo 96720
961-6627

Travel agents, tour operators, tourism

Captain Beans Cruises
73-4800 Kanalani St
Kailua-Kona 96745
329-2955

Jack's Tours Inc
226 Kanoelehua Ave
Hilo 96720
961-6666

Kona Zodiac
74-425 Kealakehe Pkwy
#16
Kailua-Kona 96740
329-3199

Roberts Hawaii Tours
73-4800 Kanalani St #200
Kailua-Kona 96740
329-1688

Roberts Hawaii Tours
16-188 Melekahiwa
Keaau 96749
966-5483

Kauai top companies

Agriculture

Pioneer Hi-Bred/Plant
Breeding
Box 596
Kekaha 96752
337-1413

Gay & Robinson
Box 156
Kaumakani 96747
335-3133

Kauai Coffee Co
Box 8
Eleele 96705
335-5497

Amfac-JMB/Lihue
Plantation
2970 Kele
Lihue 96766
245-7325

Kilauea Agronomics Inc
Box 80
Kilauea 96754
828-1761

Kauai Nursery & Land-
scaping
3-1550 Kaumualii Hwy
Lihue 96766
245-7747

Automotive

Alamo
3276 Hoolimalima Pl
Lihue 96766
246-0645

Avis Rent A Car Systems
Kauai Airport
Lihue 96766
245-3512

Budget Rent-A-Car
Systems Inc
Box 1292
Lihue 96766
245-9031

Dollar Rent A Car
3273 Hoolimalima Pl
Lihue 96766
245-3651

Hertz
3250 Hoolimalima Pl
Lihue 96766
245-3356

King Auto Center Inc
4330 Kukui Grove St
Lihue 96766
245-4788

Contractors

Shioi Construction Inc
4023 Halau
Lihue 96766
245-3975

Construction, building supplies

Akita Enterprises
3018A Aukele St
Lihue 96766
245-5344

Aloha Lumber Co
4-1525 Kuhio Hwy
Kapaa 96746
822-9818

Hale Kauai
Box 1749
Lihue 96766
245-4014

Detective, security

Freeman Guards
4347 Rice #104
Lihue 96766
246-9433

Diversified

Princeville Corp
Box 3040
Princeville 96722
826-3040

Electric

Kauai Electric-Citizens
Utility
4463 Pahee St
Lihue 96766
246-4300

Financial institutions

Bank of Hawaii
445 Rice St
Lihue 96766
245-6761

First Hawaiian Bank
4423 Rice St
Lihue 96766
245-4028

Kauai Community FCU
4434 Hardy
Lihue 96766
245-6791

Hotels, resorts

Aston Kauai Beachboy
Hotel
4-484 Kuhio Hwy
Kapaa 96746
822-3441

Aston-Poipu Kai Resort
1565 Pee Rd
Koloa 96756
742-7424

Embassy Vacation
Resort
1613 Pee Rd
Koloa 96756
742-2823

Hanalei Bay Resort
5380 Honoiki Rd
Hanalei 96714
826-6522

Holiday Inn Sun Spree
Resort
3-5920 Kuhio Hwy
Kapaa 96746
823-6000

Hyatt Regency Kauai
1571 Poipu Rd
Koloa 96756
742-1234

Islander on the Beach
Hotel
4-484 Kuhio Hwy
Kapaa 96746
822-7417

Kauai Coconut Beach
Resort
Box 830
Kapaa 96746
822-3455

Kauai Hilton & Beach
Villas
4331 Kauai Beach Dr
Lihue 96766
245-1955

Kauai Lagoons Resort
Company
Box 3330
Lihue 96766
241-6020

Kauai Marriott
3610 Rice St
Lihue 96766
245-5050

Kauai Sands Hotel
420 Papaloa Rd
Kapaa 96746
822-4951

Outrigger Kauai Beach
4331 Kauai Beach Dr
Lihue 96766
245-1955

Princeville Hotel
5520 Ka Haku Rd
Princeville 96722
826-9644

Sheraton Kauai Resort
2440 Hoonani Rd
Koloa 96756
742-1661

Shinwa-Kauai Lagoons
Resort
3351 Hoolaulea Wy
Lihue 96766
241-6099

Wailua Bay Resort
3-5920 Kuhio Hwy
Kapaa 96746
245-3931

Medical care

Kauai Medical Clinic
3-3420 Kuhio Hwy
Lihue 96766
245-1500

Hale Omao Inc
4297C Omao Rd
Lawai 96765
742-7591

Wilcox Memorial Hospital
3420 Kuhio Hwy
Lihue 96766
245-1100

Kauai Veterans Memorial
Hospital
4643 Waimea Canyon Rd
Waimea 96796
338-9431

Samuel Mahelona
Memorial Hospital
4800 Kawaihau Rd
Kapaa 96746
822-4961

Real estate

Cliffs At Princeville
3811 Edward Rd
Princeville 96722
826-6219

Cliffs Club Island Owners
Assn
3811 Edward Rd
Princeville 96722
826-6219

Pahio Resort
Box 3099
Princeville 96722
826-6549

Suite Paradise
1941 Poipu Rd
Koloa 96756
742-6464

Recreation

Kauai County YWCA
3094 Elua St
Lihue 96766
245-5959

Kiahuna Golf Club
2545 Kiahuna Plantation
Dr
Koloa 96756
742-9595

Poipu Bay Resort Golf
Course
2250 Ainako St
Koloa 96756
742-8711

Restaurants

Beach House Restaurant
5022 Lawai Rd
Koloa 96756
742-1424

Gaylord's Restaurant
3-2087 Kaumualii Hwy
Lihue 96766
245-9593

JJ's Broiler
3416 Rice St
Lihue 96766
246-4422

Jolly Roger Restaurant
4-484 Kuhio Hwy
Kapaa 96746
822-3451

Kapaa Fish & Chowder
House
4-1639 Kuhio Hwy
Kapaa 96746
822-7488

Roy's Poipu
2360 Kiahuna Plantation
Koloa 96756
742-5000

Tip Top Motel Cafe &
Bakery
3173 Akahi
Lihue 96766
245-2333

Retail: grocers

Big Save Inc
Box 68
Eleele 96705
335-3145

Big Save Inc
1105 Kuhio Hwy F
Kapaa 96746
822-4971

Big Save
4469 Walalo Rd
Eleele 96705
335-3127

Big Save
9861 Waimea Rd
Waimea 96796
338-1621

Big Save Inc
444 Rice St
Lihue 96766
245-6571

Koa Trading Co Inc
2975 Aukele
Lihue 96766
245-6961

M & K Distributors Inc
3148 Oihana St
Lihue 96766
245-7976

Safeway
4-831 Kuhio Hwy
Lihue 96766
822-2464

Star Market
Kukui Grove Center
Lihue 96766
245—7777

Retail: general merchandise

K Mart
4303 Nawiliwili
Lihue 96766
245-7742

Longs Drug Stores
3-2600 Kaumualii Hwy
Lihue 96766
245-7771

Sears Roebuck and Co
3-2600 Kaumualii Hwy
Lihue 96766
246-8301

Wal Mart
33-300 Kuhio Hwy
Lihue 96766
246-1599

Retail: other

Borders Books & Music
4303 Nawiliwili Rd
Lihue 96766
246-0862

Liberty House
3-2600 Kaumualii Hwy
Lihue 96766
245-7751

Liberty House
3-2600 Kaumualii Hwy
Lihue 96766
245-7751

Schools

Kauai Community College
3-1901 Kaumualii Hwy
Lihue 96766
245-8311

Keiki Oaloha Head Start
Ctr
Box 1027
Lihue 96766
245-7287

Telecommunications

GTE Hawaiian Telephone
Co
4040 Halau
Lihue 96766
246-3225

Transportation

Kauai Commercial Co Inc
1811 Leleiona St
Lihue 96766
245-1985

Travel agents, tour operators, tourism

Kauai Island Tours Inc
2960 Aukele
Lihue 96766
245-4777

Polynesian Adventure
Tours
3113B Oihana
Lihue 96766
246-0122

Regal Travel Inc
4180 Rice St #108
Lihue 96766
245-5682

Roberts Hawaii Tours
3-4567 Kuhio Hwy
Lihue 96766
245-9558

Trans Hawaiian Services
3601 Ahukini Rd
Lihue 96766
245-5108

Maui top companies

Agriculture

Hawaiian Commercial &
Sugar
Box 266
Puunene 96784
877-0081

Kihei Gardens and
Landscape
Box 1058
Puunene 96784
244-3804

Maui Pineapple Company
870 Haliimaile Hwy
Makawao 96768
572-7211

Maui Pineapple Company
Rural Route 1-445
Lahaina 96761
669-6201

Pioneer Mill Co
380 Lahainaluna Rd
Lahaina 96761
661-3106

Wailuku Agribusiness Co
Inc
255 E Waiko Rd
Wailuku 96793
244-9570

Automotive

Alamo Rent-A-Car Inc
905 W Mokuea Pl
Kahului 96732
871-6235

Avis Rent A Car
1979 S Kihei Rd
Kihei 96753
871-7575

Budget Rent-a-Car
865 W Mokuea Pl
Kahului 96732
871-8811

Cutter of Maui
260 Hana Hwy
Kahului 96732
877-2066

Dollar Rent-A-Car
946 E Mokuea Pl
Kahului 96732
877-2731

Hertz Rent-A-Car
850 Mokauea
Kahului 96732
877-5167

Island Dodge
110 Hana Hwy
Kahului 96732
877-0031

Valley Isle Motors
221 S Puunene Ave
Kahului 96732
877-3673

Building cleaners

Highwork Unlimited Inc
910 Honoapiilani Hwy
Lahaina 96761
667-2617

P W C Hawaii Corp
910 Honoapiilani #3-A
Lahaina 96761
661-3760

Business services

Employers Options
80 Puunene Ave #101
Kahului 96732
877-6555

Interium Health Care
Inc
360 Papa Pl #205
Kahului 96732
877-2676

Computer

Maui High Performance
Computing Center
550 Lipoa Pkwy
Kihei 96753
879-5077

Contractors

Fong Construction Co
495 Hukilike #4
Kahului 96732
877-6501

Rimrock Paving Co
381 Huku Lii Pl 201
Kihei 96753
875-4589

Goodfellow Bros Inc
381 Huku Lii Pl #202
Kihei 96753
879-5205

Dorvin D Leis Co Inc
202 Lalo St
Kahului 96732
877-3902

Hygrade Electric Co
793 Alua St
Wailuku 96793
242-1484

Wasa Electrical Service
Inc
861 Eha St
Wailuku 96793
242-9764

Construction, building supplies

Eagle Hardware
270 Dairy Rd
Kahului 96732
873-2275

Maui Home Supply
400 Hana Hwy
Kahului 96732
877-0011

Detective, security

Burns International
Security
270 Hookahi St #210
Wailuku 96793
244-7579

Freeman Guards
900 Eha #201
Wailuku 96793
244-7052

Diversified

Maui Land and Pineapple
Co
120 W Kane
Kahului 96732
877-3351

Electric

Maui Electric Company
210 Kamehameha
Kahului 96732
871-8461

Financial institutions

Bank of Hawaii
27 Puunene Ave
Kahului 96732
871-8250

First Hawaiian Bank
20 W Kaahumanu
Kahului 96732
873-2275

Hotels, resorts

Aston Wailea Resort
3700 Wailea Alanui Dr
Kihei 96753
879-1922

Aloha Resorts International
10 Hoohui Rd
Lahaina 96761
669-0420

Classic Resorts
50 Nohea Kai Dr
Lahaina 96761
661-8192

Destination Resorts Hawaii
3750 Wailea Alanui Dr
Kihei 96753
879-1595

Diamond Resort Hawaii
Corp
555 Kaukahi St
Kihei 96753
874-0500

Embassy Suites Resort
104 Kaanapali Shores Pl
Lahaina 96761
661-2000

Embassy Vacation Resort-
104 Kaanapali Shores Pl
Lahaina 96761
661-1900

Four Seasons Resort
3900 Wailea Alanui Dr
Kihei 96753
874-8000

Grand Wailea Resort Hotel
3850 Wailea Alanui Dr
Kihei 96753
875-1234

Hotel Hana Maui
Box 9
Hana 96713
248-8211

Hyatt Regency Maui Hotel
200 Nohea Kai Dr
Lahaina 96761
661-1234

Kaanapali Alii
50 Nohea Kai Dr
Lahaina 96761
667-1400

Kaanapali Beach Hotel
2525 Kaanapali Pkwy
Lahaina 96761
661-0011

Kapalua Bay Hotel &
Villas
1 Bay Dr
Lahaina 96761
669-5656

Kea Lani Hotel
4100 Wailea Alanui
Kihei 96753
875-4100

Kula Lodge
Haleakala Hwy
Kula 96790
878-5135

Lahaina Shores Beach
Resort
475 Front St
Lahaina 96761
661-4835

Maui Beach Hotel
170 W Kaahumanu Ave
Kahului 96732
877-0051

Maui Coast Hotel
2259 S Kihei Rd
Kihei 96753
874-6284

Maui Eldorado
2661 Kekaa Dr
Lahaina 96761
661-0021

Maui Islander
660 Wainee St
Lahaina 96761
667-9766

Maui Kaanapalli Villa
45 Kai Ala Dr
Lahaina 96761
667-7791

Maui Park Aston
3622 L Honoapiilani Hwy
Lahaina 96761
669-6622

Maui Lu
575 S Kihei Rd
Kihei 96753
879-5881

Maui Marriott Hotel
100 Nohea Kai Dr
Lahaina 96761
667-1200

Maui Prince Hotel Corp
5400 Makena Alanui
Kihei 96753
874-1111

Maui Schooner
980 S Kihei Rd
Kihei 96753
879-5247

Maui Seaside Hotel
100 W Kaahumanu Ave
Kahului 96732
877-3311

Napili Kai Beach Club
Hotel
5900 Honoapiilani Hwy
Lahaina 96761
669-6271

Papakeea Oceanfront
3543 Lower Honoapiilani
Hwy
Lahaina 96761
669-4848

Pioneer Inn
658 Wharf St
Lahaina 96761
661-3636

Renaissance Wailea
Beach
3550 Wailea Alanui Dr
Kihei 96753
879-4900

Ritz Carlton Kapalua
1 Ritz Carlton Dr
Lahaina 96761
669-6200

Royal Lahaina Resort
2780 Kekaa Dr #203
Lahaina 96761
661-3611

Sands of Kahana
4299 Lower
Honoapiilani Hwy
Lahaina 96761
669-0400

Sheraton Maui Hotel
2605 Kaanapali Pkwy
Lahaina 96761
661-0031

Wailea Resort Co
161 Wailea Ike Dr
Kihei 96753
879-4461

Westin Maui
2365 Kaanapali Pkwy
Lahaina 96761
667-2525

Whaler on Kaanapali
Beach
2481 Kaanapali Pkwy
Lahaina 96761
661-4861

Manufacturing: food

Haleakala Dairy
55 S Wakea Ave
Kahului 96732
877-5541

Maui Pineapple Co
120 W Kane
Kahului 96732
877-3351

Maui Soda & Ice Works
918A Lower Main
Wailuku 96793
244-7951

Media

Maui Publishing Co
100 Mahalani St
Wailuku 96793
244-3981

TCI of Hawaii
350 Hoohana St
Kahului 96732
871-7303

Medical care

Clinical Labs of Hawaii
1831 Wili Pa Loop
Wailuku 96793
244-5567

Hale Makua
472 Kaulana St
Kahului 96732
877-2761

Kaiser Permanente
Medical Group
80 Mahalani
Wailuku 96793
243-6000

Kula Hospital
204 Kula Hwy
Kula 96790
878-1221

Maui Medical Group Inc
2180 Main St
Wailuku 96793
242-6464

Maui Memorial Hospital
221 Mahalani St
Wailuku 96793
244-9056

Non-profits

Ka Lima O Maui
95 Mahalani
Wailuku 96793
244-5502

Maui Economic Opportu-
nity
189 Kaahumanu Ave
Kahului 96732
871-9591

Real estate

Baldwin Pacific Corp
55 S Wakea Ave
Kahului 96732
877-5544

Kapalua Land Co
1000 Kapalua Dr
Lahaina 96761
669-5622

Maui Realty Co Inc
1885 Main St #404
Wailuku 96793
244-9036

Recreation

Gold's Gym
850 Kolu St #A-3
Wailuku 96793
242-5773

Grand Waikapu Country
Club
2500 Honoapiilani Hwy
Wailuku 96793
244-7888

Kaanapali Golf
2530 Kekaa Dr
Lahaina 96767
667-4126

Kapalua Golf Club
300 Kapalua Dr
Lahaina 96761
669-8044

Makena Golf Course
5415 Makena Alanui
Kihei 96753
879-3344

Pukalani Country Club
360 Pukalani St
Pukalani 96768
572-1314

Royal Kaanapali Golf
Courses
Kaanapali Resort
Lahaina 96761
661-3691

Wailea Golf Course
100 Wailea Golf Club Dr
Kihei 96753
875-5111

Restaurants

Aloha Cantina
839 Front St
Lahaina 96761
661-8788

Avalon Restaurant & Bar
844 Front St
Lahaina 96761
667-5559

BJ's Chicago Pizzeria
730 Front St
Lahaina 96761
661-0700

Buzzs Wharf
1449 Front St
Lahaina 96761
661-0151

Chart House
1450 Front St
Lahaina 96761
661-0937

Chart House
500 N Puunene Ave
Kahului 96732
877-2476

Chart House
100 Wailea Iki Dr
Kihei 96753
879-2875

Cheeseburger In Paradise
346 Front St
Lahaina 96761
661-0830

Denny's Restaurant
840 Wainee St
Lahaina 96761
667-7898

Denny's Restaurant
2463 S Kihei Rd
Kihei 96753
879-0604

Five Palms Beach Grill
2960 S Kihei Rd
Kihei 96753
879-2607

Hard Rock Cafe
900 Front St
Lahaina 96761
667-7400

Host Maui Marriott Airport
Restaurant
Kahului Airport
Kahului 96732
877-5858

Hula Grill
2435 Kaanapali Pkwy #P
Lahaina 96761
667-6636

International House of
Pancakes
70 E Kaahumanu
Kahului 96732
871-4000

International House of
Pancakes
Azeka Place Shopping
Center
Kihei 96753
879-3445

Jameson's Grill & Bar
200 Kapalua Dr
Lahaina 96761
669-5653

Kobe Japanese Steak
House
136 Dickenson St
Lahaina 96761
667-5555

Lahaina Bubba Gump
Shrimp Co
889 Front St
Lahaina 96761
661-3111

Leilanis on the Beach
2435 Kaanapali Pkwy
Lahaina 96761
661-4495

Longhi's Cafe
888 Front St
Lahaina 96761
667-2288

Luigis Pasta & Pizzeria
Maui Mall Shopping Ctr
Kahului 96732
871-9521

Mamas Fish House
799 Poho Pl
Paia 96779
579-9248

Moose McGillycuddy's
844 Front St
Lahaina 96761
667-7758

Old Lahaina Cafe &
Luau
1287 Front St
Lahaina 96761
667-1998

Planet Hollywood Inc
744 Front St
Lahaina 96761
667-7877

Plantation House
Restaurant
2000 Plantation Club Dr
Lahaina 96761
669-6299

Roy's Kahana Bar &
Grill
4405 Honoapiilani Hwy
Lahaina 96761
669-6999

Rusty Harpoon
2435 Kaanapali Pky #-1
Lahaina 96761
661-3123

Ruth's Chris Steak
House
900 Front St
Lahaina 96761
661-8815

Sam Choy's Kahului
Kaahumanu Shopping
Center
Kahului 96732
893-0366

Tony Roma's
1819 S Kihei Rd
Kihei 96753
875-1104

TS Restaurants
2530 Kekaa Dr #G-2
Lahaina 96761
667-4810

Retail: clothes

Maui Clothing Co Inc
1000 Limahana Pl #N
Lahaina 96761
667-2647

Retail: general merchandise

Costco
540 Haleakala Hwy
Kahului 96732
877-5241

J C Penney
Kaahumanu Center
Kahului 96732
877-4004

Longs
Kaahumanu Shopping
Center
Kahului 96732
877-0041

Longs Drug Store
1221 Honoapiilani Hwy
Lahaina 96761
667-4384

K Mart
424 Dairy Rd
Kahului 96732
871-8670

Liberty House
Kaahumanu Shopping
Center
Kahului 96732
877-3361

Sears
275 W Kaahumanu Ave
Kahului 96732
877-2221

Shirokiya
Kaahumanu Shopping
Center
Kahului 96732
877-5551

Retail: grocers

Ah Fook's Supermarket
Kahului Shopping Ctr
Kahului 96732
877-3308

Armstrong Produce
651 Ilalo St
Wailuku 96793
242-5854

Foodland
Pukalani Terrace Center
Pukulani 96768
572-0674

Foodland Market
Kaahumanu Shopping
Center
Kahului 96732
877-2808

Foodland Super Market
840 Wainee St
Lahaina 96761
661-0975

Foodland Super Market
1881 S Kihei Rd
Kihei 96753
879-9350

Minit Stop Stores Of Maui
123 Hana Hwy
Paia 96779
579-9227

Nagasako Super Market
Box 755
Lahaina 96767
661-0985

Ooka Super Market
1870 Main St
Wailuku 96793
244-3931

Pukalani Superette
15 Makawao Ave
Pukalani 96788
572-7616

Safeway
1221 Honoapiilani Hwy
Lahaina 96761
667-4392

Safeway
170 E Kamehameha Ave
Kahului 96732
877-3377

Star Market
1310 S Kihei Rd
Kihei 96753
879-5871

Star Super Market
Maui Mall
Kahului 96732
877-3341

VIP Foodservice
Box 517
Kahului 96732
877-5055

Retail: other

Honolua Surf Co
1000 Limahana Pl #C
Lahaina 96761
667-9781

Maui Chemical & Paper
Co
875 Alua
Wailuku 96793
244-7311

Sports Authority
270 Dairy Rd
Kahului 96732
871-2558

Borders Books & Music
270 Dairy Rd
Kahului 96732
877-6160

Sultan Co
727 Wainee St #103
Lahaina 96761
667-5873

Lahaina Galleries Inc
728 Front St
Lahaina 96761
667-2152

Schools

Maui Community College
310 Kaahumanu Ave
Kahului 96732
984-3500

Seabury Hall
480 Olinda Rd
Makawao 96768
572-7235

St Anthony Jr Sr High
School
1618 E Main St
Wailuku 96793
244-4190

Science: research

Boeing North American
535 Lipoa Pkwy #200
Kihei 96753
875-4500

Rockwell International
Corp
535 Lipoa Pkwy #200
Kihei 96753
874-4500

Telecommunications

GTE Hawaiian
Telephone Co
60 S Church St
Wailuku 96793
242-5131

Transportation

Kahului Trucking &
Storage
140 Hobron Ave
Kahului 96732
877-5001

Tri Isle
860 Eha
Wailuku 96793
244-1800

Travel agents, tour operators, tourism

Blue Hawaiian Helicopters
105 Kahului Heliport
Kahului 96732
871-8844

Maui Ocean Center
192 Maalaea Rd
Maalaea 96753
875-1962

Maui Tropical Plantation
1670 Honoapiilani
Wailuku 96793
244-7643

Ocean Activities Ctr
1847 S Kihei #203
Kihei 96753
879-4485

Polynesian Adventure
Tours
273 Dairy Rd
Kahului 96732
877-4242

Roberts Dispatch
Box 247
Kahului 96732
871-4838

Roberts Hawaii Tours
747 Kaonawai Pl
Kahului 96732
871-6226

Trans Hawaiian Services
711 Kaonawai Pl
Kahului 96732
877-7308

Trilogy Excursions
180 Lahainaluna Rd
Lahaina 96761
661-4743

Molokai top companies

Agriculture

Akea Farms Inc
Box 1050
Kaunakakai 96748
567-6228

Molokai Ranch
Box 259
Maunaloa 96770
552-2741

Hotels, resorts

Kaluakoi Hotel & Golf
Club
Box 1977
Maunaloa 96770
552-2555

Medical care

Molokai General Hospital
Box 408
Kaunakakai 96748
553-5331

Lanai top companies

Hotels, resorts, tourism

Experience At Koele
Keomoku Hwy
Lanai City 96763
565-4653

Lanai Company Inc
421 10th St
Lanai City 96763
565-3803

Lodge At Koele
Keomuku Hwy
Lanai City 96763
565-7300

Manele Bay Hotel &
Resort
Box 310
Lanai City 96763
565-7700

My job search daily contacts

Date_____

Name	Company	Phone	Referral Company/Phone	Results

My job search daily contacts

Date_____

Name	Company	Phone	Referral Company/Phone	Results

My job search daily contacts

Date_____

Name	Company	Phone	Referral Company/Phone	Results

My job search daily contacts

Date_____

Name	Company	Phone	Referral Company/Phone	Results

About the Author

Rich Budnick received a B.A. Degree in History and Political Science from UCLA, and a M.A. Degree in Government from California State University, Sacramento.

His varied career includes work in the Governor's Communications Office, in addition to public relations positions with the Hawaii State Labor Department, and the Maui County Mayor's Office. He also worked as a Legislative Assistant for the California State Legislature.

As a freelance writer, Budnick has completed assignments for many Hawaii businesses, and written magazine articles for local and national publications.

Budnick is a consultant on book self-publishing, and organized the Honolulu Writers Conference to help aspiring authors learn the business of writing and publishing. As an editor and consultant, he has helped many people publish their books.

This is his fourth book as an author and a self-publisher. Other books by Rich Budnick are:

▶ Hawaiian Street Names: The Complete Guide to Oʻahu Street Names (with Duke Kalani Wise)

▶ Maui Street Names: The Hawaiian Dictionary and History of Maui Street Names (with Hokulani Holt-Padilla)

▶ Stolen Kingdom: An American Conspiracy.